HISTORICAL TOURS

CHARLESTON

HISTORICAL TOURS

CHARLESTON

Trace the Path of America's Heritage

LEE DAVIS PERRY

Globe
Pequot

Guilford, Connecticut

Globe
Pequot

An imprint of The Rowman & Littlefield Publishing Group, Inc.
4501 Forbes Blvd., Ste. 200
Lanham, MD 20706
www.rowman.com

Distributed by NATIONAL BOOK NETWORK

British Library Cataloguing in Publication Information Available

Library of Congress Cataloging-in-Publication Data

Names: Perry, Lee Davis, author.
Title: Historical tours Charleston : trace the path of America's heritage / Lee Davis Perry.
Description: Guilford, Connecticut : Globe Pequot, 2018. | Includes bibliographical references and index.
Identifiers: LCCN 2018006850 (print) | LCCN 2018009524 (ebook) | ISBN 9781493023646 (e-book) | ISBN 9781493023639 (pbk. : alk. paper)
Subjects: LCSH: Charleston (S.C.)—Tours. | Charleston (S.C.)—Guidebooks. | Historic sites—South Carolina—Charleston—Tours. | Historic sites—South Carolina—Charleston—Guidebooks.
Classification: LCC F279.C43 (ebook) | LCC F279.C43 P47 2018 (print) | DDC 917.57/91504—dc23
LC record available at https://lccn.loc.gov/2018006850

Printed in the United States of America

All the information in this guidebook is subject to change. We recommend that you obtain current information before traveling.

Contents

The Confederate Defenders Memorial honors those who fought for the Confederate Army during the American Civil War.

Introduction: Welcome to Charleston

Charleston is a land of history and the home of Revolutionary statesmen. This is a city of gallantry, glory, folly, and pain—where democracy was nurtured and secession proclaimed. This is where, very early on, beauty was deemed as important as survival, whatever the cost. Pride was encouraged. Families were sacrosanct, and God was dutifully acknowledged in mind and matter.

To gain a greater understanding of Charleston's colorful story, let's begin with a bit of geography. Two rivers, the Ashley and the Cooper, bind the historic Peninsula, the heart of Charleston's identity. Despite whatever else those rivers have meant to Charleston and its people over time, the waters effectively impounded the eighteenth-century city. This watery restraint forced all real growth and change northward—pushing it upward, spilling it over onto neighboring lands. Even today, neighborhoods that were built "east Cooper" or "west Ashley" always carry the unspoken phrase "of the Peninsula" and bear indirect witness to the old city's powerful presence.

Charleston offers several tours (walking, bus, trolley and horse-drawn carriage tours) for tourists looking to take in the sights downtown.
© ISTOCK.COM/CSFOTOIMAGES

View of Charles Towne.
COURTESY OF LIBRARY OF CONGRESS

The natural containment of the Ashley and Cooper Rivers (effectively protecting the Peninsula from change) had an accomplice in the Lowcountry itself. The southeastern third of South Carolina is physically low, close to sea level, prone to swampland, marsh, and innumerable shallow creeks and streams. The land was hostile toward early settlers and planters, and it was costly to railroad builders and almost every other developer. It didn't welcome growth, and it resists change to this day.

The sociopolitical passions and turbulent economies that made Charleston such a fascinating place 200 years ago are still very much with us

TIMELINE

1670 Founding of Charles Towne colony
1680 Colony moved to a safer location on Peninsula
1690 City walls and bastions are built
1719 Revolt leading to establishment of South Carolina as a province of British Crown
1728 & 1732 Devastating yellow fever epidemics
1739 Stono Rebellion takes place near Charleston
1740 Major fire along the waterfront
1752 Great Hurricane of 1752

1773 The Charleston Museum is established
1780 British Siege of Charleston
1783 Newly liberated city changes name to "Charleston"
1785 The College of Charleston is chartered
1786 State capital moves from Charleston to Columbia
1788 Land ceded to the city by the Pinckney family for The City Market
1791 President George Washington spends a weeklong visit in the city

1800 Santee Canal connects Columbia to Charleston
1822 Denmark Vesey slave uprising
1824 The Medical College of South Carolina is founded
1830 The "Best Friend of Charleston" train establishes first regular rail service
1838 The Great Fire
1843 The Citadel receives its first class of cadets
1861 Outbreak of American Civil War
1862 Robert Smalls commandeers CSS *Planter*

today. In the eighteenth and early nineteenth centuries, this Lowcountry land and its waters spawned a rich, romantic, fragile culture largely based on a single cash crop—rice. Any real understanding of the Lowcountry and its ethic includes an appreciation for rice and the major role it played in the development of the area. The immense wealth generated by this plantation economy left not only a legacy of architectural gems and treasure trove of fine decorative arts, but also the heavy burden of an unjust slavery system. The cheap labor fostered an incredible cost of human lives and labor to construct, develop, maintain, and harvest massive amounts of this crop for shipment to foreign ports. The expanding slave market resulted in several uprisings, and polarized sentiments among the landowners to protect this way of life leading up to secession and the American Civil War. Post-war socio-economic woes further contributed to segregation and isolation of the newly freed African Americans.

The Reconstruction years also kept all Charlestonians economically depressed and isolated into the early twentieth century while America pushed westward into its destiny. Charleston and its captive Peninsula effectively stayed behind surrounded by its many coastal distractions. Perhaps the city's hardships ironically contributed to her timelessness.

If anything is more remarkable than Charleston's softly pastel colors, cobblestone streets, graceful church spires, and elegant old homes with their exquisite interiors—it has to be the fact that any of it still exists at all. No other colonial city has suffered so many calamities as often as Charleston. Time after time, fire left vast areas of the city in ashes. The city was bombarded during war twice—once by the British during the American Revolution and again by Northern cannons in the American Civil War. Mother Nature has

1863	Charge of the 54th Massachusetts Infantry on Fort Wagner
1886	The Great Earthquake
1901	South Carolina Interstate and West Indian Exposition opens
1904	Construction of U.S. Navy Yard
1906	Hampton Park created
1920	Founding of the Preservation of Old Dwelling Houses (now the Preservation Society of Charleston)
1925	"The Charleston" dance craze spreads across the country
1931	City of Charleston establishes the "Old and Historic District"
	protecting a twenty-three-block area
1947	Historic Charleston Foundation established
1969	Charleston Hospital Strike
1970	Charles Towne Landing State Historic Site opens
1977	Debut of Spoleto Festival USA
1982	Construction of Charleston Place sparks a revitalization of the downtown shopping district
1985	Avery Research Center for African American History and Culture established
1989	Devastation by Hurricane Hugo
1990	Waterfront Park created
1996	Charleston Naval Base closure
2000	Raising of the CSS *Hunley* submarine after 136 years underwater
2005	Arthur Ravenel Jr. Bridge opens becoming the longest cable-stayed bridge in North America
2007	Sofa Superstore fire takes the lives of nine firefighters
2015	Emanuel A.M.E. Church massacre of nine parishioners
2015	Gaillard Center reopens after an extensive $142 million renovation

Handmade sweetgrass baskets, a Gullah traditional craft, on display at Charleston's City Market.
© ISTOCK.COM/KIRKIKIS

repeatedly hurled fierce hurricanes and tornadoes at the city, and it has been cracked and shaken periodically by terrible earthquakes.

And yet, as you walk through the large and little streets south of Calhoun, you find them lined with fascinating architectural relics of the past. It's hard to imagine that much of what looks so timeless and permanent today could so easily have been swept away by any number of man-made disasters or devastating natural happenstances.

After the U.S. Navy Yard military presence was established in 1904, Charleston stepped up to meet the demands of a country heading into two world wars. As the economy improved so did Charleston's awakening of the historical and cultural treasures still in her possession. A few early visionaries rose up to meet the challenge of architectural preservation and restoration. Destruction in the name of progress was forestalled, and establishment of the country's first historic district in 1931 offered legal protection to back it up. The hard work and the regularly tested courage of today's preservation organizations carry on that effort. At the same time in the 1920s and 1930s, the Charleston Renaissance emerged as the visual, literary, and performing arts found expression that had lain dormant for decades. This recognition and celebration of Charleston's uniqueness set the stage for a new economic boost—tourism.

As prosperity seeped in, and Spoleto Festival USA named Charleston as the site for its international arts festival in 1977, a second even larger reawakening took place. Charleston was discovered and has become one of the most popular tourism destinations in the world. Isolated? No longer. Timeless? Splendidly so. This is Charleston: a place, a people, and a unique perspective on the world.

This moss-draped avenue of Live Oaks can be found on the grounds of Boone Hall Plantation.
© iSTOCK.COM/ WERKSMEDIA

Key Figures in Charleston's History

Cassique The Cassique or Chieftain of the Kiawah tribe of Native Americans who inhabited the Lowcountry of South Carolina was instrumental in aiding the first colonists to settle here. He had previously traded with the settlers in Cape Fear, North Carolina, and had even sent his nephew as an emissary to England with explorer Captain Robert Sandford in 1666. Cassique met with both Sandford and Dr. Henry Woodward as they explored the region for the Lords Proprietors, the eight Englishmen who had been granted lands in the new colony by King Charles II. He and his tribe were friendly to the English and encouraged the newly arrived settlers to establish their colony on a site on the west bank of the Ashley River (then called the "Kiawah") at Albemarle Point in 1670. The struggling colonists benefited greatly from trade and their good relationship with the Kiawah. The Kiawah also lent their support against threatening attacks by the Spanish. Two statues, one wooden and one bronze, commemorate the Indian chief at Charles Towne Landing State Historic Site, the original settlement location. The names also live on at the Kiawah Island resort, just outside of Charleston, and at one of their golf courses called Cassique.

Septima P. Clark (1898–1987) As a teacher educated at Avery Normal Institute in Charleston, Septima Clark participated in the NAACP's successful drive to change state law allowing black teachers to teach in the city of Charleston for the first time in 1920. She also became involved in the federal court case ruling that equally qualified black and white teachers had to receive equal compensation in 1945. At the Highlander Folk School in Tennessee, active in the civil rights movement, Clark wrote school pamphlets, such as *A Guide to Action for Public School Desegregation*. She also recruited and encouraged several other future leaders such as Rosa Parks, who made her famous stance by not giving up her seat on the bus in Montgomery, AL. Dr. Martin Luther King Jr. and the Southern Christian Leadership Conference (SCLC) recognized Septima Clark's contributions. In 1961 she became the director of education for the SCLC under Andrew Young, working with the Citizenship School Program which he considered the base on which the whole civil rights movement was built. She became known as

This 1955 photograph features Septima Clark (left) seated beside Rosa Parks (right) at the Highlander Folk School in Monteagle, TN.
COURTESY OF LIBRARY OF CONGRESS

the SCLC's "mother conscience" and was fully supportive of Dr. King's push for civil disobedience in a peaceful, nonviolent manner. The Septima P. Clark Expressway, a section of U.S. 17 connecting the east and west parts of the Peninsula, was dedicated in 1978.

Susan Pringle Frost (1873–1960) Spurred to action by a threat of demolition to the Joseph Manigault House (1803) and other historic structures in the old city, Susan Pringle Frost led the movement that formed the Preservation of Old Dwelling Houses in 1920. Many challenges ensued that tested the mettle of the group resulting in some exciting wins and tragic losses of historic properties. But this groundwork led to legal protection in the form of the nation's first Historic District Zoning Ordinance, adopted in 1931. Now called the Preservation Society of Charleston, the organization continues to keep a watchful eye and vocal presence in the ongoing battle between preservation and modernization, helping to preserve Charleston's treasure trove of historic architecture for future generations.

Edwin Dubose Heyward (1885–1940) Charleston's own DuBose Heyward wrote the legendary 1925 novel, *Porgy,* which inspired a renaissance of artistic effort in and about the city and its people. The story is based on the life of a poor, crippled black street vendor and his tragic love for an abused, drug-addicted woman. The novelist's playwright wife, Dorothy, co-wrote the successful stage play that opened on Broadway in 1927. None other than George Gershwin felt *Porgy* was just the vehicle he was looking for to create a new art form: the American folk opera. The world-famous work known as *Porgy and Bess* was produced by New York's Theatre Guild in 1935. Since then, the opera has played all over the world, including in Milan's prestigious La Scala.

Jonathan Lucas (1754–1821) Lucas, a millwright from England arrived on the coast of South Carolina and soon set his mechanical mind on the problem the area's rice planters faced of cleaning and preparing their rice for export. Previously, a strenuous and time-consuming hand process by slaves to collect the grain and remove the hull and brown bran layer (which would turn rancid during shipment to foreign ports) was the norm. Initially Lucas harnessed waterpower to turn millstones and mechanized mortar and pestles to hull the rice, later making further improvements to use tidal water to power mills working automatically day and night. Earlier, man-and-animal-powered mills might beat out a mere three barrels of rice a day, but Lucas' water-powered mills, run by only three people, could produce an average of one hundred barrels a week. Lucas's process rapidly propelled the rice industry to the forefront of the area's economy for more than a century. The vast wealth it generated is evident in the elegant plantation mansions, grand town houses, and gardens embellished with the finest European furnishings and imported luxuries available, many of which draw and support the booming tourism industry today.

Eliza Lucas Pinckney (1722–1793) At the tender age of sixteen, Eliza Lucas assumed the role of managing her family's plantations due to her father's military commitments back in the West Indies. She diligently took control and corresponded with her father reporting on her progress. In 1739 she received a package of seeds from Major Lucas requesting that she try to cultivate indigo, a crop he had learned was grown successfully in Jamaica. After much trial and error, subsequent years of planting yielded results. She was able to harvest and process the crop to produce the deep-blue dye so in demand in England for the Royal Navy's uniforms and other textiles. From this tenuous beginning, indigo became one of South Carolina's major profitable exports in the eighteenth century, second only to rice.

Colonel William Rhett (1666–1722) Born in London, Rhett arrived in Charles Towne in 1694. He was commissioned Vice Admiral of the Colonial Navy by the governor of Carolina to command a naval defense flotilla that successfully repelled the Franco-Spanish invasion in 1706. He perhaps is best known for his capture of the notorious "Gentleman Pirate," Stede Bonnet, and his crew, who were subsequently tried and hung at White Point in 1718. This very public execution helped put an end to the piracy off Charleston's coast that had plagued the city for many years. Colonel Rhett served Charles Towne in many other capacities as Commissioner of Fortifications and of Indian Trade, building a state house, governor's house, Free School, and sea wall. He also held the positions of Colonel of the Provincial Militia, Receiver General of the Lords Proprietors, and Surveyor and Comptroller of His Majesty's Customs for Carolina and the Bahamas. In 1712 he built his personal residence at 54 Hasell Street, which is thought to be Charleston's oldest dwelling.

His Legacy in Stone
In St. Philip's Churchyard, Colonel Rhett's gravestone reads in part:
Here rests the body of Colonel William Rhett Late of this Parish, Principal Officer of his Majesties Customs in this Province: He was a Person that on all occasions promoted the Publick good of this Colony, and several times generously and successfully ventured his Life in defense of the same."

Mayor Joseph P. Riley, Jr. (1943–) Longtime mayor of Charleston (1975-2015), Joe Riley led the city through a period of great growth and change. A fifth generation Charlestonian, Riley grew up in a city that was on the brink of development, but still had a low profile in the business, tourism, and cultural sectors. His vision, hard work, and leadership propelled the city forward. A few of his major accomplishments include Charleston Place, a $75 million hotel and retail center covering five blocks between King and Meeting Streets, which led to revitalization of the downtown shopping district. Riley Waterfront Park was the result of acquiring unattractive land along the Cooper River for many years and transforming it into a beautiful five-acre public space with a long pier, floating dock, and signature pineapple water fountain. Riley also helped attract Spoleto Festival USA, a world-class arts festival, to Charleston in 1977, placing the city on the national and international arts scene. More Peninsula waterfront improvement came in the form of the South Carolina Aquarium, which opened in 2000 after seventeen years of delays and now one of the state's top attractions. He also deftly navigated Charleston through some difficult times such as the closure of the U.S. Navy base, resulting in a loss of 30,000 area jobs, the devastation of Hurricane Hugo, the Sofa Superstore fire that killed nine firefighters, the racially-motivated killing of nine parishioners of Emanuel A.M.E. Church, and severe flooding across the city in 2015.

Philip Simmons (1912–2009) The lacy wrought-iron gates, grills, and balconies seen throughout Charleston punctuate the city's eloquent architectural statement. Many of them are original eighteenth-century works still in situ and proud survivors of a nearly lost art. But Charleston's wrought-iron artwork, thanks to a man named Philip Simmons, is still being practiced and being taught to young artisans. Born in 1912 in the city's Mazyck-Wraggborough neighborhood, Philip Simmons is an example of Charleston's rich heritage in the arts passed on through the African-American community since the days of slavery. His works have long been recognized for their fine sense of scale, balance, and craftsmanship and have been exhibited in major museums and galleries throughout the United States. Mr. Simmons was a recipient of the American Folklife Award,

Examples of Simmons's wrought-iron work can be found all over Charleston, like this Egret Gate at 2 St. Michael's Alley, Charleston. WIKIMEDIA COMMONS the highest honor bestowed on folk artists in America. Today, more than 300 documented works by Philip Simmons—gates, fences, railings, and window guards—are scattered throughout Charleston. They meld handsomely with the surviving antique works and add a meaningful continuum to the city's architectural and aesthetic history.

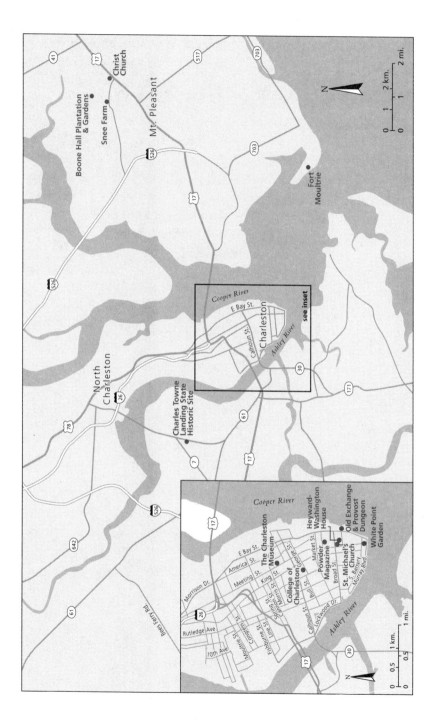

Tour 1: Charles Towne to Charleston: Colonial Settlement to Liberated City of the New Nation

1670–1799

With cultural roots as deep and colorful as the surrounding blue-green waters, Charleston is a rich mixture of early English, Scottish, Irish, French, Spanish, German, Swiss, Santo Domingan, African, Native American, and Caribbean influences.

While each of these cultures left its mark on the city in a unique way, no influence was stronger than that of the British. Archaeologists tell us countless generations of Native Americans lived on and around the land now called Charleston before the first permanent English settlers arrived, but little remains of their occupation outside of the archaeological record in the ground itself. The first English settlers, arriving in the spring of 1670, were adventurers coming to lands granted by King Charles II to eight Lords Proprietors, who claimed ownership of the "Carolinas"—presumably extending from the Atlantic to the shores of the Pacific.

As the settlers navigated into what is now Charleston Harbor, they passed enormous mounds of bleached, white oyster shells at the tip of a peninsula, where two rivers met and named the area Oyster Point. Seeking higher ground, the colonists sailed farther up one river to a high bank they called Albemarle Point and established the first crude encampment there. They dutifully named the new settlement Charles Towne for King Charles II. The two rivers, called the Kiawah and Etiwan by local tribes, were renamed the Ashley and Cooper, in honor of one of the Lords Proprietors, Anthony Ashley Cooper, Lord Shaftesbury.

The original settlement area is now a South Carolina state park called Charles Towne Landing State Historic Site. A decade later, because of their need for protection, the Charles Towne colonists were drawn back to the Oyster Point peninsula between the two rivers—clearly a more defensible location. Here, the foundations of what is now Charleston were first laid. By 1719, the colonists were tired of being exploited by the proprietary government, and friction ensued. This resulted in the colonists coming under even more discipline from the English crown, which meant forced allegiance to a series of appointed royal governors. This troublesome governmental entity stayed in place for the colonists until the American Revolution.

In 1725, the British sent over a plan for the new settlement called the "Grand Modell," intending to guide the development of 600 prime acres on the peninsula to become a proper town. Amazingly, traces of that early English plan are still evident in the plan of today's Charleston Peninsula.

Owing to the great success of this busy English port and its merchant-planter aristocracy, the town soon became a small city. To many, the eighteenth century will always be Charleston's golden age. Early travelers to this thriving colonial port took back to Europe impressive stories about Charles Towne's elegant architecture, wealthy citizenry, and sophisticated lifestyle. Indeed, during these heady, pre-revolutionary years, rice and indigo from the plantations were shipped out to eager markets all over the world. In exchange, hundreds of boatloads of enslaved Africans were brought to Charleston to ensure a cheap labor force to work the land. In stark contrast to this grim exchange, the arts flourished, and Charles Towne was considered the brightest jewel in England's colonial crown.

Many of the seeds of the American Revolution found fertile ground here in the Carolina Lowcountry. Political passions ran high, and once war broke out, there were many high-profile Charlestonians deeply involved on both sides of the issue. Actually, the first decisive American victory during the revolution occurred at the Battle of Fort Sullivan

Map showing the rivers and harbor during the Siege of Charleston, printed from the *Atlas of the Battles of the American Revolution* (1845). © SHUTTERSTOCK.COM/ STEVE ESTVANIK

(June 28, 1776) just outside the city. However, at first the war didn't go well. For a while, Charleston fell to the British, and this time, the city suffered the first of its two unseemly "enemy occupations." Newly liberated after the war, the city became incorporated in 1783 and adopted a new, shortened name: Charleston.

Charles Towne Landing State Historic Site

(1970). Charles Towne Landing State Historic Site was created as part of South Carolina's 300th anniversary celebration in 1970. The vast acreage is devoted to re-creating and interpreting the first English settlement in the Carolinas, which existed on this site back in 1670. Start at the visitor center that includes extensive interactive exhibits describing how settlers, slaves, traders, and Native Americans came together at this location to begin the first European Colony in the Carolinas. Along the river, you may explore a full-scale replica of a typical seventeenth-century trading vessel called the *Adventure,* docked at the landing in Old Towne Creek. The Animal Forest boasts a twenty-acre natural habitat zoo with otters, pumas, bears, bison, wild turkey, and alligators — all part of the Lowcountry landscape when settlers first arrived in the 1670s. The Settlers' Life Area, with its replica colonial buildings, is a handsome example of what early colonists saw every day. You'll see candle making, open-fire cooking, woodworking, and, depending on the season and the weather, even the colony's first printing press in action. Picnic tables, a vending area, and a gift shop are all on-site. The park is largely accessible to visitors with disabilities. Wheelchairs and strollers are available free of charge. Bicycles are available to rent or bring your own.

1500 Old Towne Rd. (between I-26 and SR 171), (843) 852-4200, southcarolinaparks.com.

The Battery/White Point Garden (1737). Few sites have afforded a better view of Charleston's 300-year history than the Battery. That seaside corner of land at the end of East Bay Street, where it turns and becomes Murray Boulevard, is now a pleasant park with statues and monuments, long-silent cannons, and spreading live oak trees. But the atmosphere hasn't always been so serene. The Battery has been a prominent feature in Charleston since the earliest days of the English settlement. Then, it was known as Oyster Point because it was little more than a marshy beach covered in oyster shells—bleached white in the Carolina sun. The peninsula was still unsettled, and the first colonial effort was farther upstream on the banks of the Ashley River at what is now called Charles Towne Landing. Later, when the settlement was moved to the much more defensible peninsula site, the point was a popular fishing area—too low and too easily flooded to be much of anything else. Charts used during the years 1708 to 1711 show only a watchtower on the site and just a few residences built nearby. Charles Towne was still a walled city at that time, the southernmost wall being several blocks north.

The area took a decidedly higher public profile about a decade later, when the pirate Stede Bonnet (pronounced bo-NAY) and his crew were hanged

English-Barbadian landowner, Stede Bonnet, was known as "The Gentleman Pirate." Throughout the decades, he and his crew captured merchant vessels along the East Coast. COURTESY OF LIBRARY OF CONGRESS

there from makeshift gallows. These executions were apparently quite effective in bringing an end to the pirate activity that had plagued the Carolina coast. The first of several real forts built on the site came along as early as 1737. This and subsequent fortifications were crudely built, however, and none lasted long against the tyranny of the sea. Another fort, this version constructed for the War of 1812, apparently gave White Point a popular new name— the Battery. The seawall constructed along East Battery (the "high" one) was built after a storm in 1885. The area's use as a park dates back to 1837, when the city rearranged certain streets to establish White Point Garden. It was from this vantage point that Charlestonians watched the battle between Confederate fortifications across the river and the small band of Union troops holed up in Fort Sumter on April 12, 1861. This, of course, was the beginning of the American Civil War. Once the war had started, this peaceful little garden was torn up and convulsed into two massive earthwork batteries— part of Charleston's inner line of defense. Although neither battery ever fired a shot, some incoming artillery rounds probably landed here during the extended bombardment of the city from late 1863 until Charleston fell in February 1865. The end of the Civil War was the end of the Battery's role in Charleston's military defense, although several subsequent wars have left poignant souvenirs behind for remembrance. Today no fewer than twenty-six cannons and monuments dot the Battery's landscape, each of which is described on a nearby plaque or informational marker. **2 Murray Blvd. (East Bay St., Murray Blvd., King St., and South Battery), (843) 724-7327, charlestonparks conservancy.org. Free.**

Heyward-Washington House (1772). This handsome, early Charleston "dwelling house" is known by two names because of two prominent Americans associated with it—one an owner, the other a distinguished guest. Daniel Heyward, a wealthy rice planter and the father of Thomas Heyward Jr., a South Carolina signer of the Declaration of Independence, built it in 1772. It is documented that the younger Heyward lived in the house until 1794. In 1791, President George Washington made a grand tour of the new nation and included Charleston on his itinerary. In anticipation of this distin-

Sunset along the Battery.
SERGE SKIBA/SHUTTERSTOCK
.COM

In Washington's diary, he recorded his visit to the property, saying, "The lodgings provided for me in this place were very good, being the furnished house of a gentleman at present residing in the country; but occupied by a person placed there on purpose to accommodate me."

guished visitor, the city rented Heyward's house for Washington's accommodations, and Heyward was thus displaced to his country house for the duration. Today the house is furnished with a magnificent collection of period antiques, especially some fine Charleston-made furniture of the eighteenth century. Look for the famous Holmes bookcase that still bears the scars of an incoming British mortar from the days of the American Revolution. This is the only eighteenth-century house museum in the city with original outbuildings (kitchen, carriage house, and outhouse) still a part of the

This unassuming brick house was home to a Declaration of Independence signer and hosted the nation's first president.
COURTESY OF LIBRARY OF CONGRESS

courtyard. You'll also find a small formal garden, in keeping with the period of the house. Heyward-Washington House was saved from destruction in the early 1920s by the Preservation Society of Charleston. It is now a National Historic Landmark owned and operated by the Charleston Museum. **87 Church St., (843) 722-2996, charleston museum.org. The Charleston Museum offers discounted combination ticket prices for adults for the museum, this house, and the Joseph Manigault House.**

Old Exchange and Provost Dungeon (1771).
A public building has stood on this site at East Bay and Broad Streets since Charles Towne was moved from its original settlement to its present location in 1680. The early settlers built their court of guard here. They imprisoned pirates and Native Americans in the building's lower level and held their town meetings upstairs in the hall. The British built the present building to create an impressive presence in the bustling colonial port. With its striking Palladian architecture, the Exchange surely did just that. It was completed in 1771 and quickly became the social, political, and economic hub of the growing city. From its steps, the independent colony of South Carolina was publicly declared in March 1776. During the revolution, the building was converted to a British prison, where signers of the Declaration of Independence were to be held. In 1788, the convention to ratify the U.S. Constitution met in the building, and President George Washington was lavishly entertained here several times during his Southern tour. From 1815

The Old Exchange and Provost Dungeon was built between 1769 and 1771.
© DENTON RUMSEY/ SHUTTERSTOCK.COM

to 1896, the building served both the Federal and Confederate governments as the Charleston post office. In 1913, Congress deeded the building to the Daughters of the American Revolution of South Carolina. During an excavation of the dungeon in 1965, part of the original seawall of Charles Towne was discovered. Today, the Old Exchange and Provost Dungeon is leased to the state of South Carolina and open to the public as a museum. **122 East Bay St., (843) 727-2165, (888) 763-0448, oldexchange.org.**

St. Michael's Church (1752–1761). While St. Philip's can claim to be the oldest congregation in Charleston, St. Michael's lays claim to having the oldest church structure. There is some mystery as to which the actual architect of St. Michael's might have been, but there's no question that this magnificent edifice is one of the great treasures of the city. The church has remained essentially unchanged over the centuries, with the exception of a sacristy added in 1883. However, the structure has undergone major repairs several times because of natural and man-made disasters. In the earthquake of 1886, the steeple tower sank

St. Michael's Bells: How Sweet the Sound

Among the most arresting sights and sounds of Charleston are the bells of St. Michael's Church at the corner of Meeting and Broad Streets. They ring every quarter hour in a melodic cascade of tones that sound the same today as when they were first installed in 1764. The eight bronze bells made their first of several long journeys to Charleston across the Atlantic from Whitechapel Foundry of London, England, where they were cast earlier that same year. Prior to the American Revolutionary War, the bells were rung in defiance of the British Crown, voicing the city's strong protest against the Stamp Act of 1765. Later, the bells were confiscated by the British and sent as a trophy of war to England.

Once brought to England, the bells ricocheted back to Charleston in 1782 via the generosity of a private investor, who objected to this unseemly interruption. Along came the American Civil War and once again the bells were considered at risk, and seven of the eight original bells were sent to Columbia, South Carolina, for safekeeping. As every Southerner knows, General Sherman chose Columbia as an artillery target, and the capital of South Carolina was burned to the ground in February of 1865. Only one tenor bell was left in Charleston in St. Michael's steeple to warn the city of encroaching danger. In 1865, the year the city fell, the bell rang dutifully until it cracked.

The following year, the vestry sent the charred bells along with the cracked tenor bell back to the Whitechapel Foundry to be recast in the original molds which miraculously still existed. Two years later, the sound of "Auld Lang Syne" and "Home Again" rang out over the rooftops of Charleston. The bells of St. Michael's had crossed the Atlantic again to be home (seemingly) at long last.

In 1989, however, Hurricane Hugo scored a direct hit on Charleston, and once more the bells were returned to Whitechapel for yet another recasting. This time the work was part of a $3.8 million restoration and repair of St. Michael's undertaken after the storm. And yes, once again, the original molds were used. The bells returned refreshed and renewed on July 4, 1993, and rang out in a day-long concert of traditional hand-wringing done in the English style.

St. Michael's Church stands on the corner opposite the Federal Building in downtown Charleston.
© ISTOCK.COM/KIRKIKIS

eight inches, and the church cracked in several places. St. Michael's was damaged by a tornado in 1935 and again in 1989 by Hurricane Hugo. During both the American Revolution and the Civil War, the spire was painted black to make it less visible as a target for enemy gunners. During his visit to Charleston in 1791, President George Washington worshiped at St. Michael's, where he sat in the Governor's Pew—so marked by a small plaque. In later years, the Marquis de Lafayette and then General Robert E. Lee sat in that same pew.

Buried in St. Michael's churchyard are several distinguished members of the congregation, including General Charles Cotesworth Pinckney, Revolutionary hero, signer of the Constitution, and Federalist presidential candidate; and John Rutledge, signer of the Constitution and member of the U.S. Supreme Court. **71 Broad St., (843) 723-0623, stmichaelschurch.net.**

Powder Magazine (1713). Only a couple of blocks from the bustling market area are the oldest public buildings in the Carolinas. The utilitarian Powder Magazine actually predates Charleston's legendary aesthetics. It was built for a time when the still-new English settlement was predominantly interested in

Take a stroll through the first fifty years of Charleston's history with the interactive museum exhibits at the newly-restored Old Powder Magazine. COURTESY OF LIBRARY OF CONGRESS

More Firepower
In August 1702, a survey of the armament in Charles Towne reported "2,306 lbs. of gunpowder, 496 shot of all kind, 28 great guns, 47 Grenada guns, 360 cartridges, and 500 lbs. of pewter shot." In his formal request for additional cannons, the royal governor requested "a suitable store of shot and powder . . . [to] make Carolina impregnable."

self-defense and basic survival. In the early years of the eighteenth century, Charles Towne was still threatened by Spanish forces, hostile Indians, rowdy packs of buccaneers, and an occasional French attack. It was still a walled city, fortified against surprise attack. In 1703, the Crown approved and funded a building to store additional armament, which was completed in 1713 on what is now Cumberland Street. The building served its originally intended purpose for many decades, but eventually, it was deemed unnecessary (or too small) and sold into private hands. This multi-gabled, tile-roofed, architectural oddity was almost forgotten by historians until the early 1900s. In 1901, it was purchased by The National Society of The Colonial Dames of America in The State of South Carolina (NSCDSC) It was maintained and operated as a small museum until 1991, when water damage, roof deterioration, and time had finally taken too high a toll. The Powder Magazine underwent a $400,000 preservation effort, its first ever. Much-needed archaeological and archival research was also done on the site. The Powder Magazine was reopened in 1997 by the NSCDSC. Inside, an interactive exhibit interprets Charleston's first fifty years—a time when it was still a relatively crude colonial outpost of the British Empire. **79 Cumberland St., (843) 722-9350, powdermag.org.**

The Charleston Museum (1773). Directly across Meeting Street from the Visitor Reception and Transportation Center is one of Charleston's finest jewels: the Charleston Museum. Because it is the oldest museum in America, founded in 1773, the

museum's collection predates all modern thinking about what should be preserved among the
artifacts of a culture. Instead, the Charleston
Museum is heir to the collected memorabilia of real
American patriots, early Charlestonian families,
and early colonial thinkers, explorers, scientists,
and planters. It is their opinion of what mattered
then, and what they thought should matter to us
today. Although the collection is housed in modern
buildings and has the benefit of modern conservation methods and enlightened interpretation, the
collection is uniquely eloquent. It speaks of a city
that already knew it was great and sought early on
to record itself for posterity. That difference alone
makes the Charleston Museum a must-see. The
museum's scope is the social and natural history of
Charleston and the South Carolina coastal region.
Objects from natural science, cultural history,
historical archaeology, ornithology, and ethnology
are presented to illustrate the importance each
had in the history of this area. The Charleston
Silver Exhibit contains internationally recognized
work by local silversmiths in a beautifully mounted
display. Pieces date from colonial times through the
late-nineteenth century. Visitors will see artifacts
from the early colonial period, while others are
from the American Civil War years. Some exhibits
focus on early Native Americans who lived in this
region. Others trace changes in trade and commerce, the expansive rice and cotton plantation
systems, and the important contributions made
by African Americans. Children will be intrigued by
the *Kidstory* exhibit with amazing things to touch,
see, and do. They'll see toys from the past, games

children played, the clothes they wore, furniture they used, and more. The photographs, ceramics, pewter, and tools reveal a very personal portrait of Charlestonians from the past. The Heyward-Washington House and Joseph Manigault House, owned and operated by the Charleston Museum, are an important part of its offering. In these appropriate settings, you'll see some of the museum's remarkable collection of antique furniture and other decorative arts. **360 Meeting St., (843) 722-2996, charlestonmuseum.org. Combination tickets for adults, which include admission for the museum and the two house museums, are available for two sites or for all three.**

College of Charleston (1700). Recognized as the first municipal college in the United States and the oldest institution of higher learning in

Randolph Hall is the main academic building on the College of Charleston campus. It is also one the of oldest college buildings still in use in the classical, colonial antebellum style.
© ISTOCK.COM/LEAMUS

South Carolina, the College of Charleston was founded in 1770. This thriving academic institution provides a liberal arts education to more than 11,000 undergraduate and graduate students today. Three original buildings made up the college for nearly 200 years. Now more than 100 buildings—from historic structures to high-tech classrooms—constitute the campus in the heart of historic downtown Charleston. Within this setting the college showcases beautiful landscaping with botanical displays for every season. The campus is always open for self-guided tours. **66 George St., (843) 805-5507, cofc.edu. Free.**

Boone Hall Plantation (1680s). Boone Hall Plantation dates back to the 1680s, when the Lords Proprietor made this sizable land grant to an early English settler, Major John Boone. During

Visitors can learn more about the history of the South's early cotton industry on the slave street and history tours at Boone Hall Plantation. Several of the original brick slave quarters still stand today.
© G ALLEN PENTON/ SHUTTERSTOCK.COM

the eighteenth and nineteenth centuries, Boone Hall was a thriving cotton plantation covering more than 17,000 acres. At one time Boone Hall was home to more than 1,000 slaves. Nine of the original slave houses still stand on the plantation's "slave street." The original Boone Hall mansion was lost in a tragic fire. The present structure dates from the mid-1930s. Admission includes the plantation house tour, the plantation coach tour (weather permitting), the slave street and history tour, *Black History in America* exhibit, a self-guided garden tour as well as seasonal educational performances, and the Butterfly Pavilion in the spring and winter months. Many special events take place here, so check their website and plan accordingly. **1235 Long Point Rd., (843) 884-4371, boonehallplantation.com.**

Snee Farm (Charles Pinckney National Historic Site) (1754). Let's begin with Charles Pinckney, the man. He began his public career at age twenty-two, when he was admitted to the South Carolina Bar and the South Carolina General Assembly. Pinckney served as one of four South Carolina delegates at the Constitutional Convention in Philadelphia. He served as governor of South Carolina, was ambassador to Spain from 1801 to 1805, and held seats in both the state and national legislature. He retired from public life in 1821 and died three years later. Originally, Snee Farm was part of a 500-acre royal grant awarded in 1698 to Richard Butler. By 1754, the farm comprised 715 acres and was purchased that year by Pinckney's father. The property was the family's "country seat" and an

Forgotten Founder

Often referred to as the "Forgotten Founder," Charles Pinckney presented his "Pinckney Draft" at the Constitutional Convention, which called for a strong central government made up of three "separate and distinct" branches. Some of his adopted contributions to the document included: a legislative branch made up of a Senate and a House of Delegates that would be responsible for "regulating the Trade with the several States as well with Foreign Nations," coining money, and establishing a post office; a judicial branch to settle matters among states and between the federal government and a state; and a president who would be commander in chief and deliver a State of the Union address. He also attached a "Bill of Rights" which provided for "the privilege of the writ of habeas corpus—the trial by jury in all cases, criminal as well as civil."

COURTESY OF LIBRARY OF CONGRESS

integral part of Charles Pinckney's life. Like many other Charleston aristocrats, Pinckney relied on slave labor (mostly imported from West Africa) to raise the "Carolina gold" (rice) that grew on Snee Farm. The present house on the remaining twenty-eight-acre site, built in the 1820s, is an excellent and charming example of the type of coastal cottage once common here in the Lowcountry. Guests will find interesting interpretive exhibits in and around the house. There's an informative twenty-minute video telling of Charles Pinckney, Snee Farm, George Washington's colonial era visit to the property, and the United States as a young, emerging nation. **1254 Long Point Rd., (843) 881-5516, (843) 883-3123, nps.gov/chpi.**

Christ Church (1726, 1788). Here's your first chance to encounter one of the Lowcountry's most charming undiscovered treasures, one of the

The current version of the church has been an active congregation since 1925.
COURTESY OF LIBRARY OF CONGRESS

little-known but much-loved chapels of ease. Millions of tourists visit the area and never even know these little testimonies to the Lowcountry's bygone plantation era still exist. Amazingly, they do exist, in various forms and in varied states of repair and use. First, however, a little background information is required. The Carolina colony was founded with the Anglican Church as its established religious force. Anglican congregations received financial assistance from the British government to construct houses of worship. These first Anglican churches also tended to benefit from the generosity of wealthy planters in their congregations. As a result, these churches were built with greater architectural sophistication than the early buildings of other religious organizations, and it's mostly these better-built, early Anglican structures that survive today as mute witnesses to the strength of religion in the early colonies and the isolation of plantation life. Christ Church Parish was one of ten parishes established by the Church Act of 1706. The following year, a wooden building was in place on this site, serving a slowly growing number of communicants. After fire destroyed the wooden building in 1725, a brick structure was completed in 1726. In 1782, British soldiers burned the church to the walls during the American Revolution, and it was rebuilt six years later. In 1865, during the American Civil War, fire all but destroyed the church again, and although it was once more rebuilt, regular services were discontinued by 1874. Finally, in 1925, caring descendants of early Christ Church Parish families restored both the structure and the congregation. Despite its long, hard struggle for survival, Christ Church is a viable, active congregation today. **2304 US 17 N., (843) 884-9090, christch.org.**

Fort Moultrie (1776 to 1947). From the earliest days of European settlement along the Eastern seaboard, coastal fortifications were set up to guard the newly found, potentially vulnerable harbors. In this unique restoration, operated today by the National Park Service, visitors to Fort Moultrie can see two centuries of coastal defenses as they evolved. In its 171-year history (1776 to 1947), Fort Moultrie defended Charleston Harbor twice. The first time was during the American Revolutionary War, when thirty cannons from the original fort drove off a British fleet mounting 200 guns in a ferocious battle lasting nine hours. This time, Charleston was saved from British occupation, and the fort was justifiably named in honor of its commander, William Moultrie. The second time the fort defended the city was during the American Civil War. For nearly two years, the Charleston forts (and the city itself) were bombarded from both land and sea. The walls of Forts Sumter and Moultrie crumbled under the relentless shelling, but somehow the forts were able to hold back the Union attacks. Today, the fort has been restored to portray the major periods of its history. Five different sections of the fort and two outlying areas each feature typical weapons representing a different historical period. Visitors move steadily back in time from the World War II Harbor Entrance Control Post to the original, palmetto log fort of 1776. **1214 Middle St., (843) 883-3123, nps.gov/ fosu. National Parks pass holders are free. Pets are not allowed.**

First Flag

Led by Colonel William Moultrie, the Second South Carolina Regiment was the principal command at the palmetto log and sand fort (later renamed Fort Moultrie in Colonel Moultrie's honor) on Sullivan's Island, and the regiment's colors became the garrison's flag. Colonel Moultrie recounted in his memoirs:

The grave of Major General William Moultrie, Sullivan's Island, South Carolina.
© DANIEL M. SILVA/SHUTTERSTOCK.COM

"It was thought necessary to have a flag for the purpose of signals: (as there was no national or state flag at the time) I was desired by the council of safety to have one made, upon which, as the state troops were clothed in blue, and the fort was garrisoned by the first and second regiments, who wore a silver crescent on the front of their caps; I had a large blue flag made with a crescent in the dexter corner, to be uniform with the troops: This was the first American flag which was displayed in South-Carolina [sic]."

This was the flag on the ramparts when the British were defeated on June 28, 1776, gaining the patriots their first major victory of the American Revolution. Later, when South Carolina seceded from the Union in 1861, the palmetto tree was added to the colors evolving into the state flag in use today.

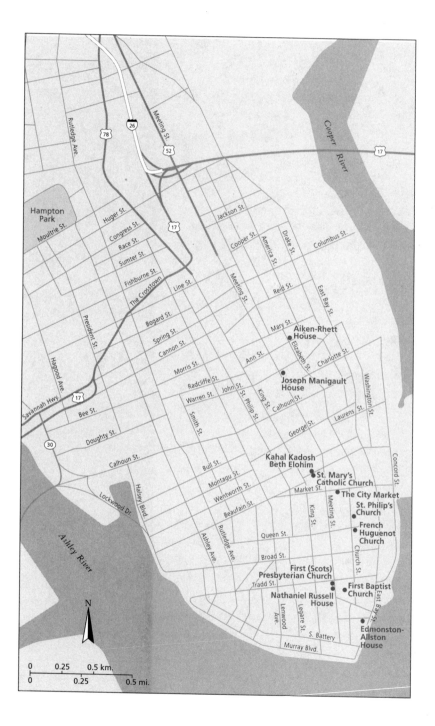

Tour 2: Antebellum Growth in Charleston's Plantation Economy, Trades, and Architecture

1800–1849

As the nineteenth century dawned, the young city of Charleston experienced an incredible building boom. Today you can still see an extraordinary number of Adam-style buildings from this remarkable period. Among them are the Joseph Manigault House at 350 Meeting St., built in 1803, and the Nathaniel Russell House at 51 Meeting St., built in 1808. Also, a number of magnificent and stately churches were erected exemplifying Charleston's religious tolerance for diverse faiths.

As cotton and tobacco were added to the plantation products earning handsome profits in the international marketplace, and even more money flowed into its thriving port, Charleston continued to grow. By the early nineteenth century, Charleston's flourishing middle class of merchant-tradesmen offered services and locally manufactured goods from small, streetfront shops. Many of these shops were clustered along what is now King Street. Some traders sold simple things such as household necessities and fresh produce brought in on wagons from outlying gardens. Others were true artisans in their own right and produced work such as early Charleston-made silver pieces and locally crafted furniture that are highly prized on the antiques market today. This flourishing "wagon trade" on upper King Street preceded the retail stores that make up the present shopping district.

The front hall of the historic
Edmonston-Alston House.
COURTESY OF LIBRARY
OF CONGRESS

Edmondston-Alston House (1825, 1838). In
1825, Charles Edmondston, another wealthy
merchant and wharf owner, built this handsome
dwelling where he could enjoy an uninterrupted
view over the expanse of Charleston Harbor.
Colonel William Alston, a rice planter, bought the
house in 1828. His son, Charles, redecorated the
house in the 1830s, favoring the fashionable Greek
Revival style. Incredibly, today's visitor can still find
many family documents, portraits, silver pieces,
and fine furnishings—including Charles Alston's
almost-intact library—in place. Much of it dates
back to the 1830s. The house is notable for its
unusual Regency woodwork, as well as its uncom-

promising views of the harbor. The intimacy and authentic details of the house may leave guests feeling as if the Alstons only recently left the property, perhaps on a visit to the country. The Middleton Place Foundation owns the Edmondston-Alston House. **21 East Battery, (843) 722-7171, edmondstonalston.com. Guided tours last thirty minutes. A combination ticket is offered with Middleton Place. Private and In-Depth tours are available by appointment.**

First Baptist Church (1822). Here is the oldest Baptist church in the South. The congregation originally emigrated from Maine to the Carolinas in 1696. The building was designed by the first American-born architect, Robert Mills, in the popular Greek Revival style. Mills didn't mince words, saying of his creation, "[it is] the best specimen of correct taste in architecture in the city. It is purely Greek in style, simply grand in its proportions, and beautiful in its detail." Wood for the solid mahogany pulpit was brought from the West Indies for the staggering sum (in 1822) of $1,000. First Baptist's fabulous organ dates from 1845 and was made by Henry Erban, a top organ maker from New York City. **61 Church St., (843) 722-3896, fbcharleston.org.**

Nathaniel Russell House (1808). Prominent shipping merchant Nathaniel Russell decided to build his great "mansion house" on Meeting Street, practically within sight of the busy wharves that produced his wealth. When his house was completed in 1808, Russell was seventy-one, and he had reportedly spent $80,000 on the project—an

Nathaniel Russell House gardens in full bloom.

enormous sum at that time. Like the Manigault house, Russell's new home was inspired by the work of English architect Robert Adam, whose delicate style was influenced by the airy classical designs only recently uncovered (literally) in the Italian excavations of Pompeii and Herculaneum. Today's visitor is immediately dazzled by the dramatic, free-flying, elliptical stairway floating up through three floors without any visible means of support. Finely proportioned, geometric rooms are furnished with another outstanding collection of Charleston, English, and French pieces, including rare china, silver, and paintings. Unlike most other Charleston house museums, the Russell House has never been through a sad period of decline and disrepair. First as a fine town house, then as the home of a South Carolina governor, and later as a school for girls and even a convent, 51 Meeting St. has always been a respected and cared-for landmark. Today it is owned and operated by Historic Charleston Foundation. **51 Meeting St., (843) 724-8481, historiccharleston.org. A combination ticket for this and the Aiken-Rhett House at 48 Elizabeth St. is available.**

First Scots Presbyterian Church (1814). Twelve Scottish families, who believed in a strict subscription to the Westminster Standards (church laws) and the Presbyterian form of church government, organized the Scots Kirk or Scots Meeting House in 1731. Their first simple structure on this site was built in 1734. It was replaced in 1814 by the present structure, which is the fifth oldest church building in Charleston. By unanimous vote of the congregation, the church bell was donated to the Confederacy in 1862 and was only recently replaced by an English bell made in 1814. Although the church was badly damaged by a fire in 1945, it was lovingly repaired. In the window over the main door appears the seal of the Church of Scotland, the burning bush, with a Latin motto that reads, *Nec Tamen Consumbatur* (*Nevertheless it was not consumed*). **53 Meeting St., (843) 722-8882, first-scots.org. Contact the office for visiting times.**

French Huguenot Church (1845). French Huguenots were followers of the sixteenth-century French reformer John Calvin. After Louis XIV revoked the Edict of Nantes (1685), there was an enormous flight of Protestants from France, many of whom came to the Carolinas. The Huguenot Church in Charleston was organized in 1681, and groups of believers arrived in this area between 1680 and

1763. In 1706, the Church Act established the Anglican Church as the official religion in South Carolina, and slowly, most Huguenot churches were absorbed into what became Episcopal congregations. The Huguenot Church in Charleston is the outstanding exception; it is the only remaining independent Huguenot congregation in America. This church was the city's first to be built (1845) in the Gothic Revival style. Edward Brickell White, a noted Charleston architect credited with popularizing the Gothic style in America, designed it. The church was damaged by shelling during the American Civil War and nearly demolished by the

The French Huguenot Church is a National Historic Landmark.
© ISTOCK.COM/MEINZAHN

1886 earthquake. Each time, it was painstakingly restored. The building underwent a major refurbishing in 1997. The church's famous Tracker organ, restored in 1967 by the Preservation Society of Charleston and the Charleston chapter of the American Organists Guild, is one of the city's true musical treasures. It is one of the last of its kind anywhere in the country. **136 Church St., (843) 722-4385, huguenot-church.org.**

St. Philip's Church (1835–1838). St. Philip's is the mother church of the Diocese of South Carolina, and for more than 300 years, this church has been a vital force in the life of Charleston. Today, there are more than 1,500 communicants. It is believed the name is derived from the Anglican parish in Barbados, the island from which many early Charleston planters came after immigration from England. The first St. Philip's was built in 1680 to 1681 on the site of what is now St. Michael's Church at Meeting and Broad Streets. A new edifice was authorized for what was considered to be the "new" gates of the city (the present site on Church Street) in 1710. This building was destroyed by fire in 1835. The present building was designed by Joseph Nyde, who was influenced by the neoclassical arches inside London's St. Martin's-in-the-Fields Church (1721) designed by James Gibbs. The history of Charleston is traceable just by reading the names of the memorial plaques around the walls of the sanctuary and in the churchyard outside. Buried here are Colonel William Rhett, officer of the Crown; Edward Rutledge, signer of the Declaration of Independence; Charles Pinckney, signer of the U.S. Constitution;

St. Philip's has been an institution in Charleston for over 300 years. Trace the history of the city by reading the names on the memorial plaques around the sanctuary, or stroll through the churchyard out back.
© ISTOCK.COM/EMILYRIVERA

and John C. Calhoun, statesman and vice president of the United States. Here, too, is the grave of DuBose Heyward, author of *Porgy* and collaborator with George Gershwin for the folk opera *Porgy and Bess.* **142 Church St., (843) 722-7734, stphilipschurchsc.org. In addition to services, visitors are welcome limited hours on Tues–Fri; call or visit the church calendar on the website for details.**

The City Market (1804). The historic City Market is one of the most colorful and popular tourist destinations in the city. The market's shopping area is flanked by busy, one-way streets (called North and South Market Streets), Meeting, and East Bay Street. The market may be one of the oldest "shopping malls" in the United States. It was built on land that Charles Cotesworth Pinckney, who was a signer of the U.S. Constitution, ceded to the city in the eighteenth century for use as a public market in perpetuity. Made up of low brick buildings that have survived hurricanes, earthquakes, tornadoes, fires, and even bombardment during the American Civil War, these sheds also were used by vendors selling fish, meat, and vegetables in bygone days. The Great Hall (1841), stretching from Meeting to Church Streets, recently underwent a $5.5 million renovation and houses a string of new specialty shops, boutiques, and eateries. Here, vendors of all types rent spaces and booths to hawk their wares including many of

Tourists shop among more than 300 vendors at one the nation's oldest public markets.
© ISTOCK.COM/FOTO-SELECT

Established 1807
CHARLESTON CITY MARKET

the local sweetgrass basket makers. The market is a must-see for every Charleston visitor, and its magic seems to lie in its eternal spontaneity. It's an ever-changing kaleidoscope of things and smells and sounds and people, who all seem to be in a carnival mood. It's different every day, and it's always the same. **188 Meeting Street, (843) 937-0920, thecharlestoncitymarket.com. Free.**

St. Mary's Catholic Church (1838–1839). Called "the Mother Church of the Carolinas and Georgia," St. Mary's was the first Catholic Church established in the English colony. Its first pastor came from Ireland in 1788. Originally known as the Roman Catholic Church of Charleston, St. Mary's officially took its present name in 1837. The Greek Revival building on the site today was consecrated in 1839, replacing an earlier edifice lost in the city's great fire of 1838. Early communicants were mostly Irish immigrants and French refugees from the West Indies. In fact, church records were kept in French until 1822. Today, the crowded church-yard contains gravestones written in Latin, French, and English representing a congregation that spanned seventeen nationalities, three continents, and two centuries. Inside, over the main altar, hangs a painting of the Crucifixion painted in 1814 by John S. Cogdell, a noted Charleston artist. The current organ is a Jardine (built in 1874 and restored in 1980) that is often featured in Piccolo Spoleto concerts held in May. **89 Hasell St., (843) 329-3237, catholic-doc.org/saintmarys. Call the office for visiting hours.**

Kahal Kadosh Beth Elohim (1840). This is the oldest synagogue in continuous use in the United States. The present congregation was organized in 1749. It is also the longest surviving Reform synagogue in the world. Beth Elohim is acknowledged as the birthplace of Reform Judaism in the United States, tracing its origins back to 1824. This is a branch of Judaism that places more emphasis on traditional religious and moral values, instead of rigid ceremonial and ritualistic detail. Cyrus L. Warner designed the present 1840-Greek Revival structure. The graceful but massive wrought-iron fence that faces onto Hasell Street dates back to the original 1794 synagogue. **90 Hasell St., (843) 723-1090, kkbe.org. Suggested donation: $10.**

Interior of the Kahal Kadosh Beth Elohim synagogue showing the architectural detail on the ceiling and East wall.

Charleston

Joseph Manigault House (1803). At the beginning of the nineteenth century, Charleston architecture was still very much dominated by what was fashionable in Mother England. This house, designed and built in 1803 by Charleston gentleman-architect Gabriel Manigault for his brother Joseph, was certainly no exception. Today it remains one of America's most beautiful examples of the graceful Adam style. Both Manigault brothers were wealthy rice planters with sophisticated tastes. Gabriel had studied in Geneva and London, where the Adam influence was at its height, and he maintained an extensive architectural library of his own. The house is distinguished by one of the most graceful staircases in the city and displays an outstanding collection of Charleston, American, English, and French furniture of the period. Don't miss the charming gate temple in the rear garden. During the 1920s, when the Manigault House was very nearly torn down in the name of progress, Gabriel Manigault's classical gate temple was used as the restroom for an oil company's service station, then on the garden site. Later, during World War II, the house served as a USO canteen for servicemen passing through Charleston's busy Navy Yard en route to battle stations overseas. Today it is a National Historic Landmark owned and operated by the Charleston Museum. **350 Meeting St., (843) 723-2996, charlestonmuseum.org. Combination tickets for adults, which include admission for the Charleston Museum and Heyward-Washington House, are available for two sites or for all three.**

Aiken-Rhett House (1818, 1833, 1857). Unlike any other house museum in Charleston, the Aiken-Rhett House is a time capsule of Charleston's history and taste. It was the home of Governor William Aiken from 1833 through 1887, and it owes most of its eerie charm to him. The structure was built in 1818 by John Robinson as a typical Charleston single house at the time. However, under the later ownership of South Carolina railroad magnate Aiken (who was governor at the time of the American Civil War), the house was drastically altered and enlarged. In 1833, it was remodeled to conform to the bold Greek Revival style popular then. Again in 1857, alterations were made, this time in the heavily ornamented Rococo Revival style that was gaining popularity in antebellum Charleston. Rococo Revival, which was popular in eighteenth-century France, is noted for curvilinear lines, as in shells, foliage, and scrolls. Here again, an uncanny amount of furnishings and other objects belonging to Governor and Mrs. Aiken can still be found, including portraits, statuary, library volumes, and elaborate chandeliers the couple brought back from Paris in the 1830s.

Governor William Aiken.
COURTESY OF LIBRARY OF CONGRESS

Much of the house is unrestored, preserved as it was when descendants of the Aiken family presented it to the Charleston Museum in 1975. As a result, the visitor can almost feel the presence of Jefferson Davis, president of the Confederacy, who was a guest in the house in 1863. You can easily picture Confederate General P. G. T. Beauregard using the house as his headquarters during the almost relentless Union bombardment of Charleston in 1864. The haunting, life-size portrait of Mrs. Aiken dressed in her finery belies the emotional and economic hardship she suffered after the war when the governor was arrested and briefly imprisoned for treason.

Another miracle of the Aiken-Rhett house is the remarkably well-preserved slave quarters and outbuildings (including stables and a privy) to the rear of the house. A high masonry wall surrounding the stable yard and slave quarters somehow managed to keep out the forces of time and change. Now owned and operated by the Historic Charleston Foundation, the Aiken-Rhett House is located only two blocks from the Charleston Visitor Center and is a must-see. **48 Elizabeth St., (843) 723-1159, historiccharleston.org. A combined ticket that includes admission to the Nathaniel Russell house is available.**

Front door of the
Aiken-Rhett House
COURTESY OF LIBRARY
OF CONGRESS

Charleston's Architectural Idiom: The Single House

You'll see a thousand examples—from grand brick or stucco structures three or four stories tall to more modest clapboard houses with one or two floors. As different as they may seem, they all share a common denominator. They all are exponents of a unique architectural invention: the Charleston single house.

In its simplest definition, the single house is one room wide (butted against the street) and two or more rooms deep. Frequently a side porch is featured—in Charleston, it's called a "piazza"—giving welcome shade and adding extra room for outdoor living. Piazzas, in turn, may also be one or multiple stories in height. All single-house piazzas, however, will have one formal opening onto the street that serves (more or less) as the property's front door.

Experts love to debate the origins of this architectural phenomenon. There are several theories. Some say the architectural roots lie in the Bahamas; others say it evolved here in Charleston as the English custom of primogeniture (whereby the eldest son inherits an entire property) began to break down. This in turn led to inherited properties being subdivided again and again into narrow, strip-like lots—the houses built on them ultimately had to conform. Another possibility is tied to residential properties being taxed according to their frontage on the street in eighteenth-century Charleston. You can choose a theory and join in the fray if you like, but genuine eighteenth- and nineteenth-century single houses are quintessentially Charlestonian. And they're a point of much deserved pride and satisfaction for those who own or live in them.

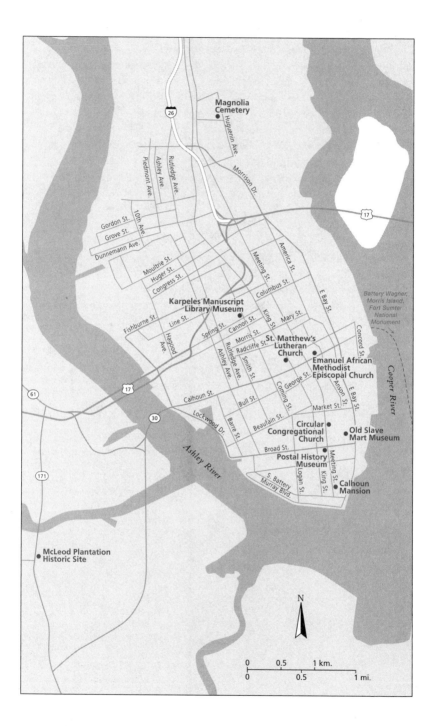

Magnolia
Cemetery

Huguenin Ave.

26

Morrison Dr.

Ashley Ave.
Rutledge Ave.
Piedmont Ave.

17

Gordon St.
10th Ave.
Grove St.
Dunnemann Ave.

Meeting St.
America St.

Moultrie St.
Huger St.
Congress St.

Columbus St.

Karpeles Manuscript
Library Museum

Fishburne St.
Line St.
Spring St.
Cannon St.
King St.
Mary St.
E Bay St.

Battery Wagner,
Morris Island,
Fort Sumter
National
Monument

Hagood
Ave.

Morris St.
Radcliffe St.
St. Matthew's
Lutheran
Church

Concord St.

Ashley Ave.
Rutledge Ave.
Smith St.

Emanuel African
Methodist
Episcopal Church

George St.

Coming St.

Anson St.
E Bay St.

61

17

30

Calhoun St.

Bull St.

Market St.

Lockwood Dr.

Barre St.

Beaufain St.

Circular
Congregational
Church

Old Slave
Mart Museum

171

Broad St.

Postal History
Museum

Meeting St.
King St.

Ashley River

S. Battery
Murray Blvd.

Logan St.

Calhoun
Mansion

Cooper River

McLeod Plantation
Historic Site

N

0   0.5   1 km.

0   0.5   1 mi.

Tour 3: The Civil War and Subsequent Struggles

1850–1900

Disputes over economics and slavery left unresolved by the young country's founding fathers had festered into a battle between the federal government and individual states by the mid-nineteenth century. In April 1861, Confederate soldiers fired on Fort Sumter in Charleston Harbor, thus signaling the start of the devastating American Civil War. After the city's second "enemy occupation," this time by Union troops, Charleston was at its lowest ebb. Years of relentless bombardment, sweeping fires, and economic starvation had taken a terrible toll on the once grand city.

Because Charleston was widely known as the "seat of secession," it is probably true that Charlestonians received especially severe punishment

Bombardment of Fort Sumter by the batteries of the Confederate States (1861).
COURTESY OF LIBRARY OF CONGRESS

during the Reconstruction years. Recovery was slow to come and sometimes halfhearted. Some say Charleston never did recuperate from the Civil War until the arrival of the Navy Yard in 1904 and the subsequent economic booms of the two world wars.

Calhoun Mansion (1876). This house museum is one of Charleston's few great Victorian-era palaces. Architecturally, it represents a brilliant expression of the Italianate style, which became extremely popular in America during the last half of the nineteenth century. This style is a rarity in Charleston's rich display of domestic architecture, possibly because when it was built in 1876, the city's economy was still devastated by the aftermath of the American Civil War. During the postwar period known as Reconstruction, very little mansion building was going on in Charleston. But the builder, George Walton Williams, a wholesale grocer and banker, was financially undaunted by the war. Unlike most wealthy Southerners, he had invested heavily in England and in the North before the war. He created what is still the largest privately-owned home in Charleston with its thirty-five rooms, 24,000 square feet of living space, twenty-three fireplaces, three-tiered piazza, Italian water gardens with fountains, and a cupola soaring ninety feet in the air overlooking Charleston Harbor. The Calhoun name comes from the fact that the builder's son-in-law, Patrick Calhoun—grandson of John C. Calhoun, "The Great Nullifier"—lived here until 1929, when he lost the house and his fortune in the stock market crash of that year. Subsequent owners failed to find a viable

Praise for Victorian-era Palace
When Mr. Williams's huge, new Charleston home was completed, newspapers in New York, Atlanta, and Charleston, immodestly described it as "the handsomest and most-complete home in the South, if not the country."

use for this venerable old mansion. It slowly slid into decline until it was finally condemned by the City of Charleston in the 1970s. A local attorney bought it and spent a considerable fortune and much of the next twenty-five years restoring its structural and artistic integrity. Today, it houses a new owner's extensive personal collection of English and American furniture of the eighteenth and nineteenth centuries—with an emphasis on Southern decorative arts. In addition, his fine collection of impressionist art, Chinese ceramics, and other objets d'art look amazingly at home in this huge Victorian-era forum originally designed to

The Calhoun Mansion was built in 1876.
© FLICKR.COM/RENNETT STOWE

create an impressive display. **16 Meeting St., (843) 722-8205, calhounmansion.net. Guided tours of the two main floors take place on the hour and half hour and by appointment. An adult must carry toddlers; no strollers allowed. A new Grand Tour covers the entire mansion including the cupola and cost $75 per person (at press time) with advance reservations.**

Postal History Museum (1896). Unknown to most of the tourists who pass through the intersection of Meeting and Broad Streets, there's a fine and fascinating little gem right there, deftly tucked into one of the corners. The Postal History Museum is a special room inside the Charleston post office showing visitors some of the interesting tidbits of postal history associated with this coastal colonial town. For instance, Charleston's first postmaster (on the job before 1694) was actually known as the city's "powder receiver." Not only was he responsible for the mail, he also collected a percentage of gunpowder from every ship that arrived for the Powder Magazine. He was required to post incoming letters in a public room in his house for thirty days and collected his commission only when the recipient picked up the letters. Imagine being in London in 1700, addressing a letter to "John Doe, Charles Towne, Carolina," and it actually getting here. This little museum is a must for philatelists or anyone else who ever wondered how eighteenth- and nineteenth-century mail was handled. It is open during regular U.S. Post Office hours, and admission is free. It's a great excuse to see Charleston's elaborately detailed 1896 post office building, the oldest continuously operating post

The Four Corners of Law

The intersection of Meeting and Broad Streets is affectionately known in Charleston as "The Four Corners of Law." The old line (mostly used these days by carriage drivers and walking-tour guides) is meant to imply that you can do literally everything legally required in life right here at this one important Charleston intersection. On the first corner you can get your mail (at the oldest operating post office building in South Carolina). On the second corner you can get married (at St. Michael's Church, built in 1761 and the place where the visiting George Washington once worshiped). On the third corner you can pay your taxes (at the Charleston County Courthouse). And

© ISTOCK.COM/KIRKIKIS

on the fourth corner—if necessary—you can get divorced (at Charleston's City Hall, built in 1801). This attitude thinly disguises the notorious Charlestonian belief that, indeed, this intersection is the center of the universe.

office in the Carolinas. **83 Broad St., (corner of Meeting and Broad Streets). Free.**

Old Slave Mart Museum (1856–1863). The one longtime local outlet for black cultural information in Charleston was the Old Slave Mart at 6 Chalmers St. At this site, reproduction slave-made wares and crafts were sold, and actual slave-era artifacts were displayed. Unfortunately, the museum failed as a privately owned tourist

The Old Slave Mart Museum offers visitors the story of slavery in the area.
© ISTOCK.COM/JCARILLET

attraction, and it closed in 1987. A year later, the City of Charleston bought the building, and later reopened it as a museum depicting the slave trading that went on here between 1856 and 1863. Among the self-guided solemn visual materials is a firsthand audio account by former slave, Elijah Green. He was born in 1843 and told his life's story in 1937 to a Works Progress Administration (WPA) writer working to preserve these memories for American history. The building encloses part of the rear yard of a tenement building, which was used for slave auctions. First called "Ryan's Mart" (after city alderman and slave profiteer, Thomas Ryan) and later, the "Mart in Chalmer's Street," this was one of several sites in this neighborhood where African-Americans were sold into slavery. It is South Carolina's only remaining slave auction house site. **6 Chalmers St., (843) 958-6467, oldslavemart.org.**

Charlestonians Embrace "Earthquake Bolts"

What are those odd iron symbols that pockmark the facades of many homes and businesses? That's the question thousands of visitors to Charleston's historic Peninsula ask when they clip-clop through the streets on carriage rides or pass by in air-conditioned buses. The answer is a poignant reminder of a devastating event, the Great Earthquake of 1886, known locally as "The Great Shake." It happened on August 31st of that year, a hot, sultry night, just after most Charlestonians had retired to bed. It shook the Holy City to its knees and was felt from the Atlantic seaboard to the Mississippi Valley, from the heart of Alabama and Georgia to as far north as Lake Michigan. Aftershocks continued for days. Ninety percent of the city's buildings were damaged, and 102 were completely destroyed. Almost all of the city's 14,000 chimneys toppled over. Experts estimate that the quake was equal to a measurement between 6.8 and 7.7 on the Richter scale.

Following the earthquake federal engineers descended upon the devastated city with recommendations aimed at preventing this tremendous loss of property (as well as lives) from ever happening again. They suggested that "all masonry walls should be securely anchored to the floor, ceiling, and roof timbers with iron anchors" threaded through the walls between the floors. Salesmen offered a variety of cast iron rods secured with decorative gib plates and screws with lion's heads, crosses, disks, and stars. Desperate Charlestonians took this advice to heart and bought the untested earthquake rods and plates by the hundreds and dutifully installed them, trusting in their supposed protective powers. Considered by most of today's structural engineers to be virtually worthless, these "earthquake bolts" remain a ubiquitous presence throughout the city awaiting the next big shake.

The portico of 13 East Battery, Charleston, collapsed during the 1886 earthquake.
COURTESY OF LIBRARY OF CONGRESS

Circular Congregational Church (1891–1892).
This church was originally called the Independent Church of Charles Towne and was established in 1681 by some of the first settlers. It was one of the first two congregations created in the settlement (the other being St. Philip's Church). The original building was of white brick and was known by locals as the White Meeting House. It is from this early euphemism that Meeting Street takes its name. That building was outgrown and replaced in 1804 by the first "Circular Church," an impressive structure designed in the Pantheon style by Charleston's famous architect Robert Mills. It is said to have seated 2,000 people, both black and white. The great fire of 1861 swept

The ruins of Circular Congrega-
tion Church
COURTESY OF LIBRARY
OF CONGRESS

across the city and took this building with it. The ruins stood mutely until the earthquake of 1886 turned them to rubble. The third (and present) building on this site was completed in 1892 and is circular in form, but Romanesque in style. The church's graveyard is the city's oldest, with monuments dating from 1695. This is the burial ground of Nathaniel Russell. **150 Meeting St., (843) 577-6400, circularchurch.org. Visitors are welcome to explore the grounds and grave-yard. Contact the office for visiting the church at times other than during services.**

Emanuel A.M.E. Church (1891). The African Methodist Episcopal Church had its beginnings in 1787 in Philadelphia with the founding of the Free African Society, based on the doctrines of Methodism and the teachings of John Wesley. The Reverend Morris Brown, a free black preacher affiliated with another Methodist church in the city, founded a similar organization in Charleston in 1791. This show of independence from the blacks led to a secession from the Methodists and the founding of three black churches in Charleston, known as the Bethel Circuit. The Emanuel A.M.E. congregation is one of those churches. The original building was in the Hampstead neighborhood in the east side of the city. By 1818, it had 1,000 members. In 1822, Denmark Vesey, a carpenter who bought himself out of slavery, laid plans in the church for a slave insurrection. Word of the rebellion leaked out, and Vesey and some of his followers were executed. The Hampstead church was burned to the ground. By 1834, all black churches in South Carolina were closed by the state legislature. During the years

The Mother Emanuel A.M.E. Church made national headlines after the mass shooting that killed nine congregation members in 2015. The congregation emerged from the tragedy as an even stronger pillar in Charleston's African-American community.
© ISTOCK.COM/STONENA7

following the Denmark Vesey incident, some of the congregation returned to white churches, but others continued the traditions of their African church and met underground. The congregation resurfaced in 1865—3,000 strong. Today's building was completed in 1891. The original gas lamps that line the sanctuary have been preserved. With seating for 2,500, "Mother Emanuel" has the largest seating capacity of Charleston's African-American congregations. **110 Calhoun St., (843) 722-2561, emanuelamechurch.org. Visitors are welcome to join the parish for worship on Sundays. Check the website for schedule.**

The Holy City

Visitors to Charleston are often confused when locals refer to their home as "The Holy City." Some even take offense thinking it in some way insults the biblical Holy Land of Jerusalem, but no such slight is intended. No one knows for sure when the nickname came into general parlance, but it's widely believed that the term was used by eighteenth-century ships captains, grateful to see solid land after a perilous ocean voyage. Another theory says it has to do with Charleston's tradition of religious tolerance, reflected in the many magnificent church spires that dominate the skyline of the lower peninsula.

St. Matthew's Lutheran Church (1872). The huge influx of German immigrants to Charleston during the first half of the nineteenth century caused the city's second-oldest congregation of Lutherans to greatly expand their house of worship. The magnificently Gothic church, with its tall, German-made stained-glass windows, was finished in 1872 with a 297-foot spire that stands taller than any other in the state. John H. Devereaux designed it. In a spectacular church fire in 1965, the spire collapsed into the street below the very point, in fact, piercing the sidewalk just to the left of the church's front door. That steeple point is still there (encased in concrete) and is commemorated by a plaque honoring the congregation's courage and determination to restore the architectural treasure. **405 King St., (843) 723-1611, smlccharleston.org. Visitors are welcome to join the parish for Sunday services; check the website for schedule.**

Karpeles Manuscript Library Museum (1983). This is one of twelve museums in the United States funded by California businessman David Karpeles. They are all nonprofit endeavors to "preserve the original writings of the great authors, scientists, statesmen, sovereigns, philosophers, and leaders from all periods of world history," according to the museum's mission statement. Scholars, educators, students, and lovers of books and manuscripts are invited to enjoy these collections free of charge. This unusual but fascinating collection is housed in the former St. James United Methodist Church (1856), one of Charleston's best nineteenth-century replicas of a classical Roman temple. Special exhibits change from time to time, but the permanent collection includes some of the rare, original writings that helped build our country's unique form of government. Among the Karpeles manuscripts is one of the four original drafts of the Bill of Rights and the Emancipation Proclamation amendment to the Constitution. **68 Spring St., (843) 853-4651, karpeles.com. For more information on exhibits or special programs, contact the museum. Admission and parking are free.**

Magnolia Cemetery (1850). One of the most telling places in all of Charleston has to be the remarkably distinctive nineteenth-century cemetery at the north end of the peninsula. Not on any contemporary beaten path, and clearly not a tourist destination, Magnolia Cemetery is the quiet, final resting place of many important Charlestonians and other players in the city's long-running and colorful drama. It is also an intriguing collection of Southern funerary art in an almost unbearably romantic setting. The site was originally on the grounds of Magnolia Umbria Plantation, which dates back to 1790 and where rice was the principal crop in the first half of the nineteenth century. By 1850, however, a 181-acre section of that land on the edge of the marsh had been surveyed for a peaceful cemetery, dedicated on November of that year. From that time on (even to the present), many of Charleston's most prominent families chose Magnolia as the place to bury and commemorate their loved ones. Many of the city's leaders, politicians, judges, and other pioneers in many fields of endeavor are interred beneath the ancient, spreading live oaks of Magnolia. Among them are five Confederate brigadier generals. There is a vast Confederate section, with more than 1,700 graves of the known and unknown. The eighty-four South Carolinians who fell at the Battle of Gettysburg are included, and the *Hunley* crew was interred there after the raising of the submarine in 2000. There

This Egyptian-revival style mausoleum in Magnolia Cemetary houses the remains of one of Charleston's prominent families.
COURTESY OF LIBRARY
OF CONGRESS

Charleston

View looking down
on Fort Sumter.
© SHUTTERSTOCK.COM/
GABRIELLE HOVEY

are literally hundreds of ornate private family plots, many of which bear famous names. You will find the monument of Robert Barnwell Rhett, "Father of Secession," U.S. Senator, Attorney General of South Carolina, and author. There's also the grave of George Alfred Trenholm, a wealthy cotton broker who served as Treasurer of the Confederacy and organized many a blockade run for the cause. Trenholm is thought by many to be the man on whom *Gone with the Wind* author Margaret Mitchell's Rhett Butler was based. **70 Cunnington Ave., (843) 722-8638, magnoliacemetery.net. Free.**

Fort Sumter National Monument (1829).
Almost every Charlestonian knows the story by heart: The year was 1861. South Carolina had seceded from the Union. And yet, just a few miles

east, there at the mouth of Charleston Harbor, Union forces were still stationed at Fort Sumter. The Confederacy officially demanded that Fort Sumter be vacated, but the North adamantly refused. At 4:30 a.m. on the morning of April 12, a mortar shell burst over the fort, fired from nearby Fort Johnson. The American Civil War had begun.

At first—largely as a matter of honor—the Union forces defended Fort Sumter. But after thirty-four hours, they surrendered. It was practically a bloodless battle—no one was killed, and only a few men were wounded. Amazingly, the Confederates held the fort for the next twenty-seven months, against what was the heaviest bombardment the world had ever seen. Over the course of almost two years, no fewer than 46,000 shells (about 3,500 tons of metal) were fired at the island fort. In the end, the Confederate troops abandoned Fort Sumter on February 17, 1865, but they never surrendered.

Today, Fort Sumter is a national monument administered by the National Park Service of the U.S. Department of the Interior. The impressive $15 million interpretive center took three years to build and adds a dramatic new dimension to the Fort Sumter experience. Here, visitors are immersed in the Fort Sumter story with interactive displays and graphics, while Park Service rangers are on hand to answer questions. Among the sights found here, is the actual thirty-three-star Garrison Flag that flew over the fort that historic first night of the Civil War. It is still accessible only by boat, and the only public tour of this tiny man-made island and world-famous fort is offered through Fort Sumter Tours, Inc. You can board the Fort Sumter tour boat at the National Park Service's facility at Liberty Square at the foot of Calhoun Street on the Cooper River or from Patriots Point in Mount Pleasant. You'll need to check in for your tour at least thirty minutes early for ticketing and boarding. Departure times vary according to the season and the weather, so call the toll-free number listed for departure information. During the busy summer season, there are usually three tours a day plus a sunset tour on Friday evenings. **340 Concord St., Liberty Square or 40 Patriots Point Rd., (843) 883-3123 (NPS), (800) 789-3678, nps.gov/fosu, fortsumtertours.com. Limited wheelchair access is available; call (843) 722-2628 for details.**

Battery Wagner, Morris Island (1863). The first Union regiment of free black soldiers, the now famous 54th Massachusetts Volunteer Infantry Regiment, fought on Morris Island during the American Civil War. The bloody battle was an undeniable

confirmation of the bravery, courage, and valor of the black soldiers and their willingness to fight for the North. Although the site is not yet memorialized formally, the island can be viewed briefly during Charleston Harbor Tours, which leave from Patriots Point in Mount Pleasant or the tour boat facility at Aquarium Wharf near the South Carolina Aquarium. What you'll see are just small hills that were originally built as artillery fortifications, a few shanties, and truck farm areas. **360 Concord St., Aquarium Wharf or 40 Patriots Point Rd., Mt. Pleasant, (800) 789-3678, spiritlinecruises.com. No tours Dec-Feb. It is recommended to arrive at least 30 minutes prior to departure time.**

Battery "B" of the last U.S. artillery active during siege operations against Fort Wagner, Morris Island, S.C.
COURTESY OF LIBRARY OF CONGRESS

McLeod Plantation. (1854) McLeod Plantation dates back to the late seventeenth century, when it was one of the first profitable farms to be established along the Ashley River system. Its fine

An interior view of the first floor west parlor of McLeod Plantation.
COURTESY OF LIBRARY OF CONGRESS

collection of antebellum buildings is considered to be among the best preserved in the American South. In addition to the main house (ca. 1854), there are barns, stables, a gin house, kitchen, and a dairy plus a street of several slave cabins. According to a census taken in 1860, there were seventy-four slaves living in twenty-six dwellings on the plantation, whose work was the cultivation of Sea Island cotton. Both Confederate and Union forces occupied McLeod during the American Civil War. The main house served as a field hospital, and it housed officers from the famous 54th and 55th Massachusetts Volunteers. It also became the main office for the Freedman's Bureau serving the James Island area during Reconstruction years. McLeod Plantation, still privately owned, was acquired in 1993 by Historic Charleston Foundation, which later worked with Charleston County Parks and Recreation to preserve and maintain this important historical site. CCPRC opened the new park in 2015, and it tells the story of the struggle and transition to freedom for enslaved people in the Lowcountry. **325 Country Club Dr., (843) 762-9514, ccprc.com. Pets and bicycles are not allowed.**

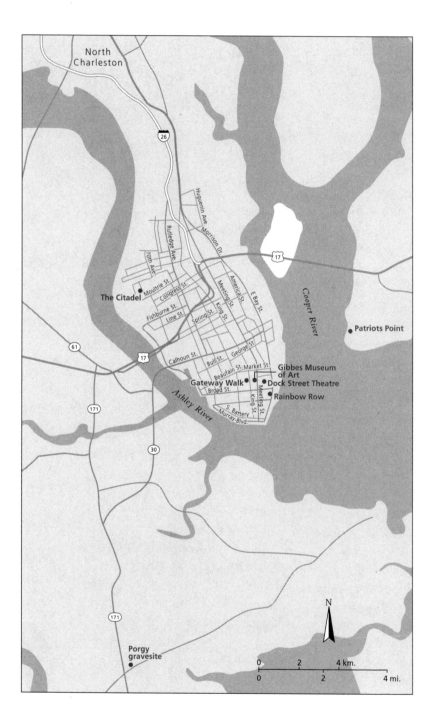

North
Charleston

26

Huguenin Ave.

Morrison Dr.

Rutledge Ave.

70th Ave.

Moultrie St.

The Citadel

Congress St.

Fishburne St.

Line St.

Spring St.

Meeting St.

King St.

American St.

E Bay St.

Congress St.

17

Cooper River

Patriots Point

61

17

Calhoun St.

Bull St.

George St.

Beaufain St.

Market St.

Gateway Walk

Broad St.

King St.

Meeting St.

Gibbes Museum
of Art
Dock Street Theatre

Rainbow Row

S. Battery

Murray Blvd.

Ashley River

171

30

171

Porgy
gravesite

N

0   2   4 km.

0   2   4 mi.

Tour 4: Cultural Renaissance and Economic Boom

1901–1950

Fires, earthquakes, hurricanes, yellow fever epidemics, and even the boll weevil threatened the health and wealth of Charlestonians during the late-nineteenth and early-twentieth centuries. After the arrival of the Navy Yard, things started looking better. Phosphate, an organic fertilizer, was mined along the Ashley River and processed in several local factories. This proved to be a significant new source of income for many old plantation families who still owned phosphate-rich lands. Other landowners converted to timber farming as the South slowly rebuilt a working economy.

It has been observed that in the most difficult of times, Charleston citizens were "too poor to paint," but they were also "too proud to whitewash." This inability to modernize maintained an almost timeless feeling throughout the city and actually worked to preserve Charleston's now legendary cache of historic homes and public buildings.

In the 1920s, a kind of artistic renaissance occurred in Charleston. The city's now-quaint architectural backdrop inspired a new generation of artists, writers, poets, and musicians who captured regional and national acclaim. At the same time, Charlestonians began to realize the aesthetic and economic value of their architectural legacy. The city's first historical preservation organizations were founded with the purpose of maintaining a number of private homes and public buildings for future posterity. Their mission never faltered—especially during the difficult Depression years of the 1930s. World War II brought another boom to Charleston, with the Navy Yard expanding to produce war materials and more job opportunities than Charleston had seen in decades.

Cabbage Row (Catfish Row). This downtown area is claimed as the inspirational setting for DuBose Heyward's 1925-book *Porgy* and for George and Ira Gershwin's beloved folk opera *Porgy and Bess,* which premiered in 1935. Cabbage Row, the scene of the story, took its name from the vegetables regularly sold from carts and windowsills by the area's black residents. Heyward named it "Catfish Row" in the book; so today a hanging sign designates it as such. Now, this section houses quaint little shops, but anyone familiar with the opera and its distinctive stage settings will readily see that this place and the alleys around and behind it could easily have been the story's original scene. Was the story based on truth? Was there ever a crippled vendor named Porgy who won, then, lost, the love of a troubled woman named Bess? Many older Charlestonians recall a poor, crippled man who lived here in the early 1920s and used a small goat cart to get around. His name was Samuel Smalls. More avid music lovers and *Porgy* fans may want to visit Smalls's grave, which is well marked in the churchyard of James Island Presbyterian Church. **1632 Fort Johnson Rd. (the intersection of Folly and Fort Johnson Roads). Look for the marker to Porgy just outside the fenced churchyard.**

Rainbow Row. Quite arguably, this is one of the most well-known and photographed sites in Charleston. And this is for good reason. This colorful series of thirteen historic Georgian row houses stretching along East Bay Street between Elliot and Tradd Streets comprise the longest group of this style of house in the country. The buildings originally fronted the Cooper River (before the land was subsequently filled in), making them prime real estate for commerce as goods arrived by sailing ships into the port city. Merchants constructing commercial buildings with storefronts to sell their wares on the ground floor and living areas above built them in the last half of the eighteenth century. Most had only exterior staircases in the rear yards to access the upper floors. After the Civil War, Charleston's economy declined so that this

Visitors can see iconic Rainbow Row via bus, car, or on foot. © ISTOCK.COM/RIVERNORTH-PHOTOGRAPHY

area fell into poor condition. In the 1920s preservationist Susan Pringle Frost purchased six of the houses to prevent their further destruction. Gradually she began residential restoration efforts and sold 99-101 East Bay to Dorothy Legge in 1931. Mrs. Legge restored her property and decided to paint her houses pastel pink inspired by a colonial Caribbean color palette. Other owners followed her lead and a "rainbow" of pastel facades emerged leading to the popular moniker, Rainbow Row. **79-107 East Bay Street. Note: These are private homes with no public entry.**

Dock Street Theatre (1809, 1937, 2010). Among Charleston's many firsts, the Dock Street Theatre is the first building in America constructed exclusively for use as a theatrical performance venue. The first theatre building was constructed on the south side of Queen (then called Dock) Street, just a little west of heavily traveled Church Street. It opened with a performance of *The Recruiting Officer* on February 12, 1736, and later, *Flora*, the first opera performance in America took place here. The theatre was said to have had a stage, pit boxes, and a gallery. Most of the original building was probably destroyed in the Great Fire of 1740.

Eventually, a second theater was constructed nearby, and an early hotel was built on the rear portion of the old theater lot in 1809. It was called the Planters Hotel, popular lodging for Lowcountry planters and their families, who would traditionally leave their plantations to be in town for the winter social season. The old Planters Hotel is the structure that was still standing, but in ruins when, in the 1930s, the New Deal's WPA rebuilt it as the theater we know today. On November 26, 1937, Charleston's own DuBose Heyward, already famous for *Porgy,* would write a special dedication to reopen a new facility. The reconstruction of the Dock Street recaptured the spirit of early Georgian theaters without intending to be an exact reconstruction, while providing a modern theater

Exterior of the Dock Street Theatre
COURTESY OF LIBRARY OF CONGRESS

capable of handling a wide variety of productions. The auditorium seats 463 people, with a pit and a parquet of thirteen boxes. The walls are paneled with natural local black cypress, and the cove ceiling has exceptional acoustic properties. Over the stage hangs a carved wood bas-relief of the Royal Arms of England (obligatory in all Georgian theaters), duplicated from an original that still hangs above the altar in Goose Creek's chapel of ease, built in 1711. The Dock Street's stage has a proscenium opening of thirty-four feet and features an apron forestage with "proscenium doors" on either side. Today's stage floor is flat, whereas the original was most likely tilted. The theatre reopened for the third time in 2010 after an extensive $19 million state-of-the-art renovation. **135 Church St., (843) 720-3968, (843) 965-4032 (box office), charlestonstage.com.**

Gibbes Museum of Art (1905). Established in 1905 by the Carolina Art Association, the Gibbes Museum of Art offers the visitor access to a distinguished and growing collection along with year-round exhibitions, educational programs, and special events. The building itself stands as a memorial to James Shoolbred Gibbes, a wealthy Charlestonian who bequeathed funds to the city of Charleston and the Carolina Art Association to create a permanent home for the association's collection. Today that rich and fascinating collection includes American paintings, prints, and drawings from the eighteenth century to the present. There are landscapes, genre scenes, views of Charleston, and portraits of notable South Carolinians. Faces associated with history (and architectural landmarks all over the Lowcountry) seem to come to life here. You'll find Thomas Middleton painted by Benjamin West and Charles Izard Manigault painted by Thomas Sully. There's John C. Calhoun painted by Rembrandt Peale, plus an outstanding collection of more than 400 exquisite, hand-painted miniature portraits of eighteenth- and nineteenth-century Charlestonians. The Gibbes also has an outstanding collection of early Japanese woodblock prints. In addition to the regular schedule of exhibitions on loan from international, national, and regional collections, the Gibbes presents major exhibitions in the visual arts during Spoleto Festival USA every May through June. Admission to the museum shop is free. The Gibbes is fully wheelchair accessible. **135 Meeting St., (843) 722-2706, gibbesmuseum.org.**

Gateway Walk (1930). In 1930, Mrs. Clelia Peronneau McGowan, president of The Garden Club of Charleston, came up with the idea for a walkway

Peek inside the iron gates for a view of some of Charleston's most luxurious private homes on this self-guided tour.
© ISTOCK.COM/MANAKIN

that would connect the city's churchyards, garden areas, and tucked-away courtyards. She was inspired by a trip to Paris, where she embraced the idea of meandering through serene gardens in the midst of a bustling cityscape. The plan was designed by noted Charleston landscape architect Loutrel Briggs and opened on April 10, 1930, to celebrate the 250th anniversary of the founding of Charleston on its Peninsula site. The self-guided walk is designated by unobtrusive plaques and footstone markers that lead through historic sites, but depart from the sidewalk viewpoint and beckon into the hidden core of four city blocks between Archdale Street and Philadelphia Alley. The stroll passes through churchyards full of fascinating old tombstones with a variety of blooming flora. It continues through the gardens of the Charleston Library Society and the Gibbes Museum of Art, which features the Governor Aiken gates, a fountain, and sculpture. Winding your way through several centuries of Charleston history, you'll discover how Gateway Walk was named for the beautiful wrought-iron gates along the way. **(To get a map start at St. John's Church office at 5 Clifford St.), Free.**

Gateway Walk Inscription
An inscription on one of the plaques attributed to Mrs. McGowan reads:

"THROUGH HAND WROUGHT GATES, ALLURING PATHS
LEAD ON TO PLEASANT PLACES,
WHERE GHOSTS OF LONG FORGOTTEN THINGS
HAVE LEFT ELUSIVE TRACES."

The Citadel (1842). Founded in 1842, The Citadel is a state-supported military college with an enrollment of more than 2,000 cadets. The original campus was located on Marion Square with the two-story Romanesque building (now renovated as the Embassy Suites Historic District) serving as the barracks.

In 1920, the college was relocated to the banks of the Ashley River with room to expand. With

a formal campus and regimented activities, The
Citadel combines academic requirements with
military training in the areas of discipline, respon-
siveness, and leadership. Almost every Friday
during the school year, the 2,000-member Corps
of Cadets marches in retreat parade or review on
Summerall Field to close out each week. In addition to family and friends, the Dress Parades are a
long-standing local and visitor favorite due to the
impressive precision of the Corps. Spectators are
welcomed—just be sure to take your seat before
3:45 p.m., when the action commences. **171
Moultrie St., (843) 225-3294, citadel.edu. The
campus is always open for self-guided tours.
Free. Call or visit the website for a schedule.**

Patriots Point Naval and Maritime Museum.
Patriots Point is the name given to a huge maritime
museum complex that consists mainly of three
World War II-era ships (permanently situated): a

The Citadel's campus is open
year-round for self-guided tours.
© ISTOCK.COM/SAILAWAY46

The retired aircraft carrier, USS *Yorktown*, is the main attraction at Patriots Point, a military museum.
© ISTOCK.COM/RIVERNORTH-PHOTOGRAPHY

submarine, USS *Clamagore,* a destroyer, USS *Laffey,* and the flagship of the museum, USS *Yorktown* (Aircraft Carrier). The *Clamagore* tour route covers the control room, berth and mess areas, engine rooms, maneuvering room, and displays of submarine warfare. A tour of the *Laffey* lets you see the bridge, battle stations, living quarters, and various displays of destroyer activities. The flight deck, hangar deck, and many of the *Yorktown* crew's living and working quarters are open to visitors. You'll find actual carrier aircraft and Vietnam-era anti-sub planes on display—twenty-six aircraft in all. Another exhibit in the complex is the true-to-scale Vietnam War Naval Support Base, showing the living conditions and work areas of a typical support base. The Cold War Submarine Memorial features a full-sized replica of a Fleet Ballistic Missile submarine with educational stations that pay tribute to those who served our country in naval submarines from 1947 to 1989. You'll also find the newly renovated and expanded Medal of Honor Museum, featuring interactive displays representing the different eras of military history in which the Medal of Honor was awarded. You'll see actual Medals of Honor and some of the artifacts related to their original recipients. Mercifully, you'll find a snack bar onboard the *Yorktown* and another in the riverside gift shop, so excited youngsters and foot-weary veterans can stop for lunch and a rest. For this complex, one of Charleston's major attractions, you'll need comfortable shoes and plenty of time. **40 Patriots Point Rd., (843) 884-2727, (866) 831-1720, patriotspoint.org.**

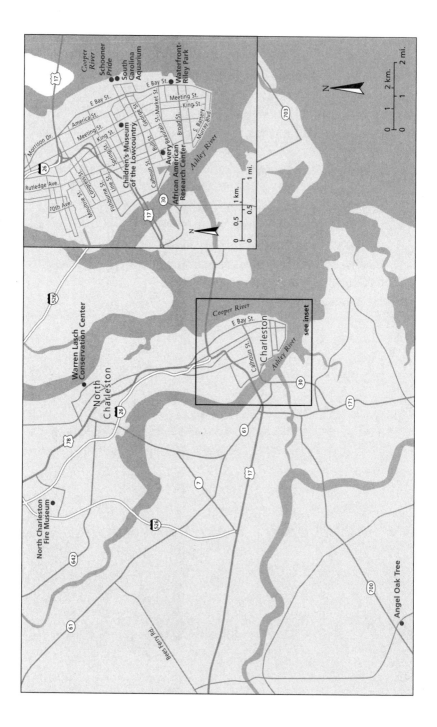

Cooper River

Schooner
Pride

South
Carolina
Aquarium

Waterfront-
Riley Park

E Bay St.

Meeting St.

King St.

S. Battery

Murray Blvd

Ashley River

E Bay St.

America St.

Meeting St.

King St.

Morrison Dr.

Children's Museum
of the Lowcountry

Avery
African American
Research Center

26

Rutledge Ave.

10th Ave.

Moultrie St.

Congress St.

Fishburne St.

Line St.

Spring St.

Calhoun St.

Bull St.

George St.

Beaufain St.

Broad St.

Market St.

30

17

N

0   0.5   1 km.

0   0.5   1 mi.

N

0   1   2 km.

0   1   2 mi.

526

Warren Lasch
Conservation Center

North
Charleston

78

26

61

7

17

526

North Charleston
Fire Museum

642

61

Baas Ferry Rd.

700

Angel Oak Tree

703

171

Cooper River

E Bay St.

Charleston

Calhoun St.

Ashley River

30

see inset

Tour 5: Remembering the Past while Embracing the Future
1951–PRESENT DAY

After World War II ended, many workers drawn here by the U.S. Navy decided to stay on and settle down. The sea, the mild weather, and a growing business climate kept pulling newcomers to the Lowcountry through the 1950s and 1960s. For most of the Cold War years, the Greater Charleston area served as the U.S. Navy's third largest homeport and the country's largest submarine base. North Charleston is currently home to the U.S. Air Force's 437th Airlift Wing. And the Marines, the Army, and Coast Guard still work to underscore the military's presence in this area.

In the 1970s, Charleston's Chamber of Commerce launched a national advertising campaign based on the simple slogan, "Charleston:

The opening ceremony of the Spoleto Festival
WIKIMEDIA COMMONS

America's Best Kept Secret." This, of course, was intended to let this cat out of the bag, and it worked splendidly. With high-profile cultural events such as Spoleto Festival USA, Southeastern Wildlife Exposition (SEWE), and the (almost always sold-out) house tours every spring and fall, the message was getting out—Charleston was a beautiful, historic, and highly desirable place to visit.

Today Charleston's expanded cultural calendar, sparkling beaches, and collection of historically significant architecture attract visitors from around the globe, and the city's remarkable preservation ethic is now a model for historic cities all over the industrialized world. According to a recent survey conducted by the Office of Tourism Analysis at the College of Charleston, over 5 million tourists visit Charleston each year, and the numbers continue to grow. Many visitors also decided to move here and make the Charlestonian lifestyle their own.

Riley Waterfront Park (1990). Just off East Bay Street in downtown Charleston, the lovely Waterfront Park is another nice picnic spot and a great place to cool your heels. Sea breezes keep the tables under the covered pier area perfect for just these pursuits. Children have fun splashing around in the pineapple-shaped fountain or getting soaked by a circular spray fountain. We've seen pictures of half a kindergarten class in one of the large swings that line the pier, a 400-foot extension into Charleston Harbor. **1 Vendue Range, Cumberland Street to North Adgers Wharf, (843) 724-7327, charlestonparksconservancy.org. Open sunrise to sunset. Free.**

Schooner Pride. Ah, here's a fantasy that is delightfully achievable. See Charleston from the water—as countless settlers and nineteenth-century immigrants saw it—from the decks of a tall ship, the Schooner *Pride*. She's eighty-four-feet long and U.S. Coast Guard-certified to carry forty-nine day passengers or twenty overnight guests. The two-hour daily cruises of Charleston Harbor and sunset and moonlight sails are offered during the spring, summer, and fall. Experienced sailors and quick learners may help with the ship, or you can simply sit back and enjoy the wind, sea, and unexpected pleasure of almost soundless propulsion. The schooner *Pride* is moored at the Aquarium Wharf on Concord Street. All tours depart from there. **360 Concord St., Aquarium Wharf, (843) 722-1112, (888) 245-9206 (Zerve Ticketing), schoonerpride.com. Call or visit the website for prices, schedules, and reservations.**

The Pineapple Fountain landscape illuminated in Waterfront Park.
© CVANDYKE/
SHUTTERSTOCK.COM

The South Carolina Aquarium also serves as the departure point for the Fort Sumter tour boat.

© ISTOCK.COM/OVIDIUHRUBARU

South Carolina Aquarium (2000). In May 2000, after years of planning, controversy, and nervous anticipation, Charleston's $69 million South Carolina Aquarium opened to rave reviews as a major new attraction in the Lowcountry. This nonprofit, self-supporting institution is dedicated to educating the public about and helping to conserve South Carolina's unique aquatic habitats. Its mission is to display and interpret the state's diverse range of habitats—from rushing mountain streams to the oceanic depths of the Atlantic. The exhibit path leads visitors through five major regions of the Southeast Appalachian Watershed as found in South Carolina—the Mountain Forest, the Piedmont, the Coastal Plain, the Coast, and the Ocean. Among the sixty exhibits in the 93,000 square-foot building are more than 6,000 plants and animals, representing more than 500 species. The aquarium is home to otters, birds, turtles, fish, venomous snakes, other reptiles and amphibians, aquatic invertebrates, and insects. The Sea Turtle Hospital tours and 4-D Theater (for an additional fee) are other popular experiences. Advance tickets are available by calling or visiting the website. **100 Aquarium Wharf, Calhoun at Concord Streets, (843) 577-3474, (800) 722-6455, scaquarium.org. Parking is available across Concord Street from the aquarium's entrance.**

Children's Museum of the Lowcountry (2003). The newest museum on the scene with a focus on kids is the Children's Museum of the Lowcountry. Located near the visitor center in the Camden Tower Sheds, this popular concept is to inspire a love of learning in children through interactive, interdisciplinary, hands-on environments and experiences in the arts, sciences, and humanities. The fun exhibits include climbing a tower in the medieval castle, sliding into the art room, painting on a mural wall, playing with water in *WaterWise*, exploring an antique fire truck, and searching for buried treasure aboard the CML's pirate ship. This immersion environment for children and their families leads to creative thinking, problem-solving skills, and confidence. Who knows what a visit here may spark? **25 Ann St., (843) 853-8962, explorecml.org.**

Avery Research Center for African American History and Culture (1990). In Charleston, the rich cultures of South Carolina's African-American communities are recognized for their unique national significance. However, the materials that document African-American culture have been widely scattered over time, and much has already been lost. The College of Charleston's Avery Research Center for African American History and Culture was established to document, preserve, and make public the unique historical and cultural heritage of this significant group for present and future generations. In October 1990, the center was established at 125 Bull St. in Charleston's historic district. Here, at long last, a growing archival collection and on-site museum could share the purpose of gathering together these valuable materials and encouraging scholarship on the subject. The research center is on the site of the former Avery Normal Institute, the local normal school (for teachers-to-be) and college preparatory school that served Charleston's black community for nearly one hundred years. There, the school produced not only teachers, but also other gifted leaders for South Carolina and the nation. Avery Normal Institute was organized in October 1865 by black minister F. L. Cardozo of the American Missionary Association for (in his words) "the education of colored children." In 1868, the school moved into the Bull Street building just five blocks west of the College of Charleston. Today, the center's archival collections are regularly used for exhibits and educational programs for the public. These activities are planned in conjunction with local and national African-American celebrations and holidays. **125 Bull St., College of Charleston, (843) 953-7609, cofc.edu/avery. Written inquiries should be addressed to Avery Research Center for African American History and Culture, 66 George St., Charleston, SC 29424.**

CSS *H. L. Hunley* (1864). In 1864, the CSS *H. L. Hunley* was the first submarine in history to successfully sink an enemy warship when it launched an attack against the Union ironclad *Housatonic* off the coast of Charleston. The *Hunley* and its eight-man crew never returned to homeport, however, and its fate remained unknown until divers located the sub in 1995. It was discovered partially buried in mud not far from the scene of its 1864 triumph. In August 2000, the *Hunley* made national headlines as it was carefully raised from its watery grave and brought back to Charleston for several years of painstaking conservation and analysis. It rests, for now, at the high-tech Warren Lasch Conservation Center on the former Charleston Navy Base, where scientists are slowly unlocking the mysteries of its disappearance, including how and when the crew died. **Warren Lasch Conservation Center, 1250 Supply St., Bldg. 225, (877) 448-6539, (843) 743-4865, ext. 10, hunley.org, etix.com. Advance reservations are suggested to view the sub in its tank and see the exhibits of its contents and technology.**

North Charleston Fire Museum (2007). Who doesn't have a natural fixation on fire, firemen, and their bravery? The North Charleston and American LaFrance Fire Museum and Educational Center addresses our infatuation with their display of over twenty meticulously restored firefighting vehicles that trace the history and evolution of firefighting in general. The 20,000-square-foot facility houses colonial-era firefighting equipment from the 1780s through a 1973 Century Series Pumper manufactured by the American LaFrance Company, who own and sponsor the $5 million collection. Many of the exhibits are interactive and hands-on, so little firefighter wannabes are free to explore and enjoy it all. A realistic simulator shows kids exactly what a firefighter sees as a fire truck races through the city. Blazing horns, vibrating seats, and flashing lights all make it seem real. Another exhibit traces the important decision-making required to successfully fight a house fire. Kids even learn how to slide down a fireman's pole, and how to exit a burning building safely. **4975 Centre Pointe Drive, (843) 740-5550, northcharlestonfiremuseum.org.**

Angel Oak (1991). Don't laugh, but we're about to suggest taking a drive to the countryside of John's Island for the sole purpose of seeing . . . a tree. That's right, a tree. It's an oak tree, but it's a very special one, a very old one, and a very famous one. The tree is called Angel Oak, and everything about it is pure Lowcountry. No visitor has really seen the Charleston area without making the trip out to the island to be summarily awed and embraced by the Angel Oak's mighty outstretched arms.

Live oak trees (*Quercus virginiana*) are native to the Lowcountry. During the eighteenth and nineteenth centuries, lumber from the live oak forests was highly valued for shipbuilding. In fact, most of the area's ancient live oaks were harvested during those two centuries.

This live oak, however, survived. Angel Oak has been reported to be hundreds of years old, although the exact age is difficult to calculate. Angel Oak is only sixty-five feet tall, yet its circumference is twenty-five-and-half feet. The area of shade under this huge canopy is an incredible 17,000 square feet, and the longest outstretched limb reaches out eighty-nine feet and has a circumference of more than eleven feet. Clearly,

Charleston

the Angel Oak is quite old. It knew the Lowcountry long before the English settlers arrived. It was already an old tree when the Kiawah tribe lived on this land and no doubt enjoyed its shade. It knows more than any of us ever will about hurricanes, wars, fires, earthquakes, and time.

The property where the Angel Oak stands was originally part of a land grant to Abraham Waight in 1717. Waight became a prosperous planter with several plantations in the Lowcountry, including the Point, where the Angel Oak stands. The property passed through generations, acquiring the Angel name when Martha Waight married a Justis Angel in 1810. The Angel family plantation was sold in 1959 to the Mutual Land and Development Corp. The City of Charleston acquired the Angel Oak property in 1991, and it was opened to the public on September 23 of that year. **3688 Angel Oak Rd., (843) 559-3496, angeloaktree.com. Free.**

The massive, sprawling Angel Oak is one of the oldest live oaks in the Lowcountry. © ISTOCK.COM/MICHAEL VER SPRILL

Charleston

Staying, Eating, and More Touring

GETTING AROUND CHARLESTON

With heavy seasonal traffic (in spring, as many as half a million visitors come to Charleston by car), seemingly constant road- and bridge-work, and a peculiar system of one-way city streets, getting around Charleston is not always simple on first try. Also, parking is always a problem. The city has made strides toward managing the situation to the benefit of both residents and tourists, with restricted parking hours in residential neighborhoods and more parking garages for public use. Metered parking spaces are limited, but convenient when you can find them. To avoid costly tickets, a parking garage is your safest bet.

Another good option to avoid the parking problem in the old historic district is for visitors to make the **Charleston Visitor Reception and Transportation Center** their first destination. Its location on 375 Meeting Street offers visitors a welcome opportunity to leave their cars behind and see Charleston's large historic district (mostly on the southern end of the Peninsula) by any of several alternative transportation options. This visitor center is the major, general information resource site in Charleston proper. Once you've taken in the city's overview of itself, it's time to go out and see the real thing. Starting here, it's very possible to "do" the city and leave your car at the visitor center lot or garage. The visitor center is open daily 8:30 AM to 5 PM except New Year's, Thanksgiving, and Christmas Day.

Public bus transportation in the area is a great way to circumvent the city's automobile congestion and parking woes altogether. The **Charleston Area Rural Transportation Authority** (CARTA) provides this service. Under CARTA's auspices is the **Downtown Area Shuttle** (DASH), a separate system generally dedicated to the transportation needs of tourists in the downtown area and historic district. Ride DASH for free downtown on Routes 210 College of Charleston/Aquarium, 211 Meeting/King, and 213 Lockwood/Calhoun all of which stop at the visitor center.

While the green DASH trolleys are not considered tour vehicles per se, their turn-of the-twentieth-century trolley look is clearly an eye catcher—and it's one way to quickly identify a DASH vehicle from the more modern-looking (yellow and green) CARTA buses that operate in the metro area. Together, CARTA and DASH offer more than twenty routes linking downtown, West Ashley, Mount Pleasant, and North Charleston. DASH trolleys and CARTA buses only stop at designated shelters, benches, and trolley stop signs located throughout the city. Call (843) 724-7420, or visit ridecarta.com for more information.

If you (plus one more passenger) just need to scoot around downtown and you're tired of hoofing it, you can summon one of the handy rickshaws that orbit the City Market area. The three-wheeled, bicycle-like wonders pedal about the streets starting at 9 AM until 2 AM seven days a week. All are "driven" by strong-winded college kids who know the city and the bicycle rules of safety. You can hail one anywhere you see it, or you can call the dispatch number at (843) 723-5685, and one will pedal to your location (approximate response time: 5 minutes). At press time, rates are about $6 one-way (for about a 10-minute ride). More information is at charlestonrickshaw.net.

SLEEPING IN THE MIDST OF HISTORY

If the Lowcountry knows a thing or two about putting up guests, it's because millions of them visit the area each year, and no one sees an end to this upward trend in sight. To accommodate these visitors, a diverse accommodations industry has evolved to meet those needs. Downtown Charleston has the greatest number and the widest variety. We have included here what we consider a sampling of good choices for people who may be looking for vastly different accommodations. We focus on downtown area hotels and motels, and a few of the more intimate bed-and-breakfasts and atmospheric inns. Travelers interested in more bed-and-breakfast options may want to visit the Charleston Bed & Breakfast Association's website, charlestonbb.com, for more detailed information and photos of member properties. All must meet certain standards of quality and service and boast innkeepers ready to share their love of Charleston with their guests.

There are also many viable lodging options in the East Cooper, West Ashley, and North Charleston areas that are generally less expensive than staying on the Peninsula. The resort islands of Kiawah and Seabrook feature an array of cottages, villas, condominiums, and private homes. For the most part, rental companies for the resorts and other traditional vacation spots (Isle of Palms,

Sullivan's Island, and Folly Beach) prefer to deal with stays of one week or longer. A friendly word of advice: Charleston attracts droves of visitors year round (there are major events scheduled nearly every month), and we strongly recommend that you make reservations well in advance. For major events like Spoleto Festival USA and holiday weekends, it's advisable to plan up to six months in advance.

Ansonborough Inn. The award-winning Ansonborough Inn is at the end of Hasell Street off East Bay. There are thirty-seven suites that have been cleverly fashioned out of a turn-of-the-century warehouse. Heart-of-pine exposed beams (measuring 12 inches by 12 feet) and locally made red brick have been incorporated into the decor to give the inn a remarkably warm feeling, even with its magnificent sixteen- and eighteen-foot ceilings. The facility's three floors are wheelchair accessible and surround an open central atrium. The suites are equipped with full kitchens, and some have lofts. There's an on-site English-style pub and rooftop bar. A twenty-four-hour monitored parking lot is available next door. One favorite amenity is the continental breakfast with fresh-baked breads, pastries, bagels plus a varied hot item. The afternoon wine and cheese social is a great pick-me-up after a long day of touring. The business traveler is treated to multiple data ports, wireless Internet, and on-site conference facilities. **21 Hasell St., (843) 723-1655, (800) 723-1655, ansonboroughinn.com.**

Belmond Charleston Place Hotel. In terms of size, Belmond Charleston Place Hotel is the granddaddy of Charleston accommodations, with 440 luxury suites and superbly appointed rooms in the massive complex in the city's downtown shopping district. The hotel, with its impressive lobby and reception area, opens into the walkway of a mini-mall that includes such famous stores as Gucci, St. John, and Godiva. The full-service European spa with its on-staff masseur and masseuse has an indoor-outdoor swimming pool among the luxury amenities. Under the auspices of Belmond Hotels, the rooms at Charleston Place have taken on the aura of sophisticated southern charm. Expect to find Italian Carrara marble vanities and walk-in showers or soaker tubs in the roomy baths. They add just that much more romance to your lodging experience. Several superb dining options are available right under the Charleston Place roof. Foremost among them is the Charleston Grill on the main floor tucked away among the shops and boutiques. **205 Meeting St., (843) 722-4900, (888) 635-2350, belmond.com/charleston-place.**

Embassy Suites by Hilton Charleston Historic District (1829). This all-suite luxury hotel is located in the historic district in what was originally The Citadel's first home (ca. 1829). Unmistakably a military building, the echoes of young cadets marching off to the Civil War still seem to bounce off these old walls. Enjoy 153 handsomely furnished two-room suites with private bedrooms and living rooms. The decor recalls the grandeur of the colonial West Indies. All guest suites open onto a stone-floored atrium with giant palms and a three-tiered fountain. Amenities include in-room wet bars, two telephones, mini-refrigerators, microwaves, complimentary Wi-Fi, complimentary cooked-to-order breakfast and beverages each evening. This is an ideal location, and just a stroll from the visitor center, the Charleston Museum, and special events in Marion Square. **337 Meeting St., (843) 723-6900, (800) 362-2779, historic charleston.embassysuites.com.**

Francis Marion Hotel (1924). Built in 1924 and beautifully renovated, the Francis Marion is now one of the city's most popular hotels. Named for American Revolutionary War General Francis Marion, also known as "the Swamp Fox," the hotel offers all the traditional services of a grand hotel—valet parking, concierge, doorman, bell service, and room service. In all, there are 235 guest accommodations ranging from rooms with two double beds to two-room king suites. All have been handsomely reappointed with custom detailing. At twelve-stories tall, the hotel affords visitors a bird's-eye view. It's near upper King Street's fast-developing shopping district, the Charleston Museum, the College of Charleston, and the visitor center. The hotel's signature restaurant, the Swamp Fox Restaurant & Bar, offers a very pleasant atmosphere on the first-floor King Street side. A complete day spa and Starbucks are on-site too. Ample parking is just next-door in a city-owned garage. **387 King St., (843) 722-0600, (877) 756-2121, francismarioncharleston.com.**

John Rutledge House Inn (1763). Built in 1763 by John Rutledge, a signer of the U.S. Constitution, the house at 116 Broad St. has been completely renovated and transformed (as part of a three-building complex) into a swanky inn with nineteen rooms in all. The house is a designated National Historic Landmark, and the National Trust for Historic Preservation named it among the top thirty-two Historic Hotels of America for good reason. George Washington himself had breakfast here and was one of many patriots, statesmen, and presidents who came to call on Mr. Rutledge. The main residence contains elaborate parquet floors, Italian marble mantels, and molded plaster ceilings. Rooms have been modernized to include private baths, refrigerators, televisions, and individual climate controls. Afternoon tea is served in the ballroom, and evening turndown service includes chocolates at bedside. Continental or hot breakfast and a newspaper are delivered to guests each morning. The Rutledge House is dog friendly for an additional fee. This inn is part of the Charming Inns of Charleston group. **116 Broad St., (843) 723-7999, (800) 476-9741, johnrutledgehouseinn.com.**

Mills House Wyndham Grand Hotel (1853). Of the city's grand hotels in the historic district, the Mills probably enjoys the oldest, grandest reputation. It is located on the corner of Meeting and Queen Streets, next door to the imposing white-columned Hibernian Hall (site of many a debutante ball and home of the Hibernian Society). Modern in its comforts and antebellum in its decor, the Mills House has always been a favorite with affluent travelers. The original Mills Hotel (ca. 1853) standing on that site was deemed unworthy of restoration in the early 1960s, so it was razed and replaced with a new, fire-safe structure taller by a couple of floors, but with lobby areas and public rooms copied from the original hotel. So exacting are the reproduced details and antebellum appointments that frequently the Mills is used as a backdrop for movies and television shows needing a period hotel setting. The beautiful courtyard, outdoor pool, and deck add a casual side to the Mills experience. The in-house restaurant and bar, called The Barbadoes Room, draws local patrons as well as the international set. You'll find live entertainment somewhere on the premises each night, and turndown service is part of the pampering. It's hard to beat the Mills for location, as it is only a stone's throw from the Four Corners of Law, the King Street antiques district, several museums and galleries, plus the bustling Market area. **115 Meeting St., (843) 577-2400, (877) 999-3223, millshouse.com.**

Two Meeting Street Inn (1890). This elegant 1890-Victorian mansion is at the intersection of Meeting Street and South Battery facing White Point Garden. Guests stay in one of nine air-conditioned rooms, each with a private bath. The rooms are all different, but each carries out the Victorian theme in every detail. A hot Southern breakfast is served in the garden or the formal dining room, depending on the weather. Or you may decide to lounge in your luxury cotton bathrobe (provided with the room) and have breakfast delivered to your guest room. Afternoon tea and evening sherry is included in the rate. Much of Two Meeting Street's charm comes from the lacy Queen Anne–style veranda stretching across the front of the inn. Its lazy ceiling fans and rocking chairs make the scene an inviting option for afternoon tea.

No credit cards. **2 Meeting St.**, **(843) 723-7322,** **(888) 723-7322, twomeetingstreet.com.**

Wentworth Mansion (1885-1887). This elegantly refurbished inn was built from 1885 to 1887 as one of Charleston's few great Victorian townhomes. Articulated in what is called the Second Empire style of architecture (after a French fashion popularized during the reign of Napoleon), it was originally the private estate of Francis Silas Rodgers. Rodgers was a Charleston cotton merchant who made a fortune in phosphate after the American Civil War. His mansion survives today as the city's most opulent ode to the long-lost Gilded Age. Remarkably unchanged, the property features twenty-one rooms and suites individually decorated and furnished with nineteenth-century antiques. All rooms have king-size beds and baths with oversize whirlpool tubs. Most have working gas fireplaces. Guests enjoy the mansion's common rooms such as the Rodgers Library, the Harleston Parlor, and the atrium-like

Historic Bed-and-Breakfasts
Historic Charleston Bed & Breakfast is a local business that has been matching guests with in-home accommodations since 1981. The reservation service books more than fifty different private homes and carriage houses within the historic district. With very few exceptions, these accommodations date from 1860 or earlier. Agents for Historic Charleston Bed & Breakfast know each property intimately. They know which ones are appropriate for children, which ones are accessible to persons with disabilities and the elderly, and they can arrange for late arrivals and special transportation. Historic Charleston Bed & Breakfast also sends out excellent pre-arrival materials, including maps and shopping and dining recommendations. Rates can be slightly higher for special events and peak weekends like Cooper River Bridge Run, Spoleto Festival USA, and New Year's. Off-season rates are, of course, lower. Mar through June and Sept through Nov are usually considered peak season. (843) 722-6606, (800) 743-3583, historiccharlestonbedandbreakfast.com.

Sun Porch—where guests savor leisurely elegant breakfasts, afternoon sherry, and evening wine and hors d'oeuvres. Local guides lead guests on tours of the city, and an on-site fine dining restaurant, circa 1886, offers seasonal specialties. With its private spa, Wentworth Mansion brings a whole new level of service to Charleston's already renowned tradition of unparalleled hospitality. **149 Wentworth St., (843) 853-1886, (888) 466-1886, wentworthmansion.com.**

POPULAR DOWNTOWN AREAS FOR DINING

Over recent years Charleston's restaurant options have mushroomed with both local establishments popping up and regional and national chains following suit. Choosing the top restaurants in Charleston is pretty close to picking your favorite child. It's nearly impossible! There are so many top-rated chefs doing incredible things with fresh, locally sourced products presented in beautifully artistic and creative ways (often in historic and always elegant venues). The national food media and the Charleston Wine + Food Festival every spring have brought the cuisine in this town to the forefront of American foodies' attention.

Here, we have mainly focused on the local ones and selected those in close proximity to the major shopping and historic sites in downtown Charleston organized into three major corridors: The City Market, East Bay Street, and King Street. Other wonderful choices exist both downtown and across the bridges, and we encourage you to wander off the main streets or explore off the Peninsula.

City Market Corridor

Anson. This elegant restaurant on Anson Street is between the City Market and the trendy Ansonborough neighborhood. Recently renovated Anson is as well appointed, as it is deserving of its reputation for fine food and good service. The nouvelle American menu includes a decadent whole crispy flounder with apricot shallot sauce that should not be missed. Other temptations include outstanding first-course shrimp and grits with bacon, roasted tomatoes, and Anson's house-ground grits. When it's time for dessert, Anson's consistently gets rave reviews. Look for their dense, moist, house-made chocolate cake. Reservations are recommended. **12 Anson St., (843) 577-0551, ansonrestaurant.com.**

Charleston Grill. This is the grande dame restaurant in Belmond Charleston Place. In this beautiful, traditionally decorated eatery, quality is the byword. Service is exuberant, for those who demand close attention, and the wine list can compete with any in the South. It isn't exactly stuffy, but the atmosphere is definitely upscale. The food is simply superb. Its nightly specials are always as billed, but the regular menu is abundant in attractive choices. Try the Northern Divine caviar or "21" Club steak tartare for starters. And the grilled domestic rack of lamb with mint chimichurri makes for a delectable entree. Desserts are announced nightly for those with a taste for excess. Live jazz on weekend evenings adds a cool balm to the well-orchestrated scene. Reservations are welcomed. **224 King St., Charleston Place, (843) 577-4522, (800) 237-1236, charlestongrill.com.**

Grill 225. When the Market Pavilion Hotel opened near the Market on East Bay Street, they promised a restaurant of distinction, and clearly, it was a promise they kept. Fashioned in the style of the great steak houses of yore, Grill 225 prides itself on garnering the freshest and highest-quality beef, veal, lamb, and seafood available. The fare is deliberately simple in its creation, proportion, flavor, and presentation—so the exceptional quality of each ingredient can (and does) carry the day. For starters, try their tuna tower, and then tackle their generous cut of prime beef or double-cut lamb chops. From the sea come jumbo lump crab cakes and, of course, lobster of almost any size you specify. If you're willing, the dessert menu tempts with banana bread pudding or flaming baked Carolina. Reservations are recommended, and they can be made online. **225 East Bay St., (843) 723-0500, grill225.com.**

Hank's Seafood Restaurant. Old-time Charleston insiders remember a place called Henry's, which was part and parcel of this city's colorful "renaissance era" in the 1920s and 1930s. It was a seafood joint down in the City Market (which was a whole lot rougher in those days), and among other distinctions, old Henry's served liquor throughout Prohibition with (apparently) no interference from the city fathers. Hearty "receipts" for seafood soups and dishes laden with cream and flavor were always offered at Henry's, and generations of Charlestonians were raised on it. Hank's is today's reincarnation of that tradition, with a lot of sophistication added to the mix. An old warehouse has been carefully outfitted with a quasi-period-looking fish-house decor without being too cute about it. And several of the old Henry's dishes have been reproduced or improved upon for patrons with modern palates, who now flock there from all over the world. This is where she-crab soup is done right (lovingly flavored with crab roe and sherry), and oysters are still served on the half-shell atop beds of crushed ice. Tackle Hank's Seafood Tower of shellfish from the oceans of the world, if you like, or try the specialties (like sea scallops or seared tuna). There are several fried seafood platters that feature a variety of old Lowcountry receipts, as well. Spirits are still high and served at Hank's willingly. Reservations are suggested. **10 Hayne St., (843) 723-3474, hanksseafoodrestaurant.com.**

Kaminsky's Dessert Café. Kaminsky's is an A-plus addition to the list of indulge-thyself Peninsula eateries. Enjoy their wonderful desserts with just the right coffees and spirits to accompany them. The handsome brick walls of the Market Street location make a backdrop for a nice showcase of art, and the cafe's intimate size contributes to its appeal. Try an exotic coffee or nonalcoholic drink with a delicious dessert. The milkshakes, for instance, are legendary. Be prepared to face a dilemma: There are 150 other choices. Relax with a martini or hot toddy. **78 North Market St., (843) 853-8270, kaminskys.com.**

The Palmetto Cafe. This restaurant is inside the large Belmond Charleston Place complex and serves breakfast and lunch in a relaxed but upscale cafe atmosphere. The breakfast buffet on Saturday and Sunday is a very elaborate event with several choices of entrées and salads, fresh vegetables and fruits, plus desserts. The garden atmosphere is particularly attractive and convenient to those staying in the hotel or shopping downtown. It falls in the pricier category, but everything is beautifully presented, and it is well worth the price on a special occasion (like your first visit to Charleston). For lunch, there's nothing like the seared scallops with grapefruit salad and yellow curry vinaigrette. Follow that with filet mignon with chimichurri sauce, and salt-roasted potatoes. This stylish restaurant also features optional courtyard dining. **130 Market St., Charleston Place, (843) 722-4900, belmond.com/charleston-place.**

Tommy Condon's Irish Pub and Seafood Restaurant. The most authentic Irish pub in Charleston, Tommy Condon's has live Irish music Wednesday through Sunday and serves a variety of imported beers and ales, such as Bass and Guinness Stout. The menu is a mixture of Irish and Lowcountry items, including shrimp and grits, seafood jambalaya, shepherd's pie, and corned beef on rye. There is a covered deck for outside dining, and an inside back dining room complete with paintings of the Old Country. **160 Church St., (843) 577-3818, tommycondons.com.**

East Bay Corridor

Blossom is another see-and-be-seen place downtown, but offers the bonus of being as affordable or extravagant as your budget allows. The cafe has indoor and outdoor dining, an in-house bakery, a cappuccino bar, and an extensive New American menu with Italian and Mediterranean influences. Each menu for lunch, dinner, and late-night dining, features pastas, seafood entrees, and gourmet pizzas from the oak-burning oven. Sunday brunch is another option here. An added bonus is free parking just next door. **171 East Bay St., (843) 722-9200, blossomcharleston.com.**

Magnolias Uptown/Down South. Magnolias tops the list of chic restaurants on the Peninsula. In fact, *Travel + Leisure* called it *"the* place in downtown Charleston." This is new American-Lowcountry cuisine, and the chef's specialties include shellfish over creamy white grits with fried spinach, and the down-South egg roll stuffed with chicken, tasso ham, and collard greens. The expansive menu will remind you of the restaurant's California and Cajun inspirations, but the atmosphere is strictly refined New South. Reservations are definitely encouraged. **185 East Bay St., (843) 577-7771, magnoliascharleston.com.**

McCrady's underwent a renovation several years ago that retains much of the old tavern's charm, but adds new space and sophistication. Edward McCrady, first owner of the building, was a Madeira importer here over 200 years ago. The dark wood and exposed brick interiors hark back to the days when George Washington reportedly supped here, and the huge fireplaces add their own charm. But the service and—most of all—the cuisine are the reasons to go there. Here, fine dining is a major event. The menu changes daily, but McCrady's serves appetizers like ember-roasted squab with charred leek and sweet potato. Sometimes there are South Carolina clams, too. For entrees, try the roasted redfish with cabbage, seaweed, and orange. But delicious variations of duck, chicken, beef, pork, and lamb are always on the menu. If you're still able, try a dessert like the carrot crémeux perhaps accompanied by a vintage Madeira. The sommelier's wine list is extensive and impressive, too. **2 Unity Alley, (843) 577-0025, mccradysrestaurant.com.**

Slightly North of Broad. In one of the many nineteenth-century cotton warehouses that line East Bay Street, there's this trendy option for S.N.O.B. types. Cute name notwithstanding, the folks here are very serious about good food. It's what they call an "eclectic lowcountry bistro" with locally sourced seafood, meats, and produce. The Carolina quail and local grouper are delicious. The express lunch of the day is a hit, too. This restaurant is a favorite of those who want to lunch with friends or have a special evening on the town. Reservations are encouraged. **192 East Bay St., (843) 723-3424, snobcharleston.com.**

King Street Corridor

39 Rue de Jean. Here's a little bit of Paris on South Carolina soil. That is, this restaurant is all about French food served in the best tradition of the brasserie genre. Located across John Street from the visitor center, "Rue" is a great place to begin a dining tour of Charleston. It's known for braised short ribs with espagnole sauce and steamed mussels available in six different presentations. If you want, a large assortment of French wines is available, but domestic labels are offered too. The full-service bar is a popular stop for locals as well as first-time visitors to the city. A favorite dessert is the crème brûlée. **39 John St., (843) 722-8881, 39ruedejean.com.**

82 Queen. This multi-award-winning restaurant has several personalities—one of which is sure to please. Exploring the eleven dining rooms at 82 Queen is an adventure in itself. The grounds include three eighteenth-century town houses, two inside bars (one full-service and one just for shots), an outside raw bar that is a very popular hangout for the after-work crowd, a partly glassed-in romantic gazebo, and outdoor tables for dining. Weekend brunch is especially nice in this pleasant atmosphere. Lowcountry seafood, beef, lamb, and fowl are specialties of their updated traditional Southern cuisine. Farm-fresh herbs and vegetables are locally grown for their kitchen. The wine list includes more than 140 selections. Reservations are encouraged. **82 Queen St., (843) 723-7591, (800) 849-0082, 82queen.com.**

Coast Bar and Grill. Tucked away on Hutson Alley behind Rue de Jean (on John Street) is this seafood restaurant making big waves with locals as well as out-of-towners. When the question arises, "Where will you find good seafood?" this is always a great answer. The menu lists dozens of options—all prepared in different as well as traditional ways. Some of the favorite coastal dishes from our own Lowcountry waters are the seared rare tuna, Carolina crab cakes, and braised grouper. A full raw bar is part of the scene, but you can order your seafood wood-grilled, steamed, smoked, or fried with a choice of ten sauces. Dessert is not to be missed here. **39-D John St., (843) 722-8838, coastbarandgrill.com.**

Fish. As the name implies, this is a small restaurant on upper King Street that's mostly about (but not exclusively dedicated to) seafood. You can count on the fact that none of the seafood brought to table will be more than thirty-six hours from its native waters. The fun decor is part of the charm. You enter through a courtyard past a fountain and discover an environment that's creative and unusual without being too cute. The menu with Asian and French influences changes seasonally, but look for the sweet chile calamari in sesame tempura batter or the clams du jour. If you're game for it, choose four items like shrimp roll, duck confit, goat cheese panini, and pork belly from their dim sum menu. You might like to try the bouillabaisse, a traditional steam pot in coconut broth, suitable for two seafood lovers. The dessert they're all talking about is the "chocolate craze" with milk chocolate mousse, peanut butter ganache, and candied peanuts. **442 King St., (843) 722-3474, fishrestaurantcharleston.com.**

Fulton Five. Fulton Five is an authentic taste of old Italy tucked away on Fulton Street, just off King Street in the heart of the antiques district. The building looks Old World enough to be European, and the alfresco dining experience is definitely continental in feel. An upstairs dining area adds another perspective on the charms of quaint and narrow Fulton Street. The menu is constantly changing with new and more exciting entrees, but if the following dishes are available, we heartily recommend them. Start with antipasto Spoleto (grilled fresh mozzarella and prosciutto rolled into a romaine leaf with balsamic and tomato vinaigrette). Next, move to the carbonara ravioli with egg, pancetta, and green peas. Then, enjoy the grilled lamb chops with Parmesan polenta, and Swiss chard. For a light, sweet touch, order a grapefruit, orange, or tangerine ice made in-house or tiramisu—the perfect finale. A fine selection of Italian and other wines is always on hand. Reservations are suggested. **5 Fulton St., (843) 853-5555, fultonfive.com.**

Halls Chophouse. Located in Charleston's hip, new Upper King shopping district, Halls Chophouse immediately racked up the awards after opening just a few years ago. This premier steak house delivers with the finest USDA prime steaks flown in from Allen Brothers of Chicago. Choose from dry aged, porterhouse, New York strip, rib eye, and filet mignon for a tender, savory, and richly textured experience. Not a beef lover? That's no problem. Halls includes roasted chicken, pork, veal, and fresh seafood on the menu, too. Vegan and vegetarian diners can find plenty to eat here as well. Halls Classic Cocktail menu stirs up the perfect accompaniment to start your evening, while taking in the live music every night. The soulful sounds of their Gospel Sunday Brunch create a memorable dining atmosphere in which to try the Lowcountry omelet or crabcake eggs Benedict. Parking is directly behind the restaurant off John Street. **434 King St., (843) 727-0090, hallschophouse.com.**

Michael's on the Alley. Serious meat lovers will embrace the high-quality cuts of USDA prime, Angus, and choice steaks, wet- or dry-aged, presented at Michael's on the Alley. The bacon Gorgonzola butter or foie gras to accompany your selection can take it to the next level. Updated menu favorites from the turn-of-the-century steak house heydays include oysters Rockefeller, shrimp cocktail, Maine lobster roll, and beef tartare. The fresh seafood, lamb, pork, and tableside salad prep are other reasons to choose to dine here for a special evening out. The wooden-clad and brick dining room walls, white tablecloths, and tufted leather banquette seating add to the classic steak house feel. At the very least share one of their enticing desserts to linger a little longer. **39 E. John St., (843) 203-3000, michaels onthealley.com.**

Vincent Chicco's. If you're looking for old-fashioned Italian-American fare, look no further. Vincent Chicco's is a new offering from the restaurant group that has successfully delivered for years at Coast and Rue de Jean nearby. Celebrating classic flavors through the handmade pastas and rich homemade sauces on their menu, popular items include appetizers like the house-made burrata cheese and the bruschetta with the house's focaccia bread and local tomatoes. The *cacao e pepe* and lamb *sugo* pastas, and the veal and chicken piccatas are some of the traditional dishes that even an Italian mother would endorse. It might be hard, but save room for dessert—the New York-style cheesecake and chocolate torte are superb. **39-G John St., (843) 203-3002, vincentchiccos.com.**

Other Downtown Dining Options

FIG. Located at the corner of Meeting and Hasell Streets, FIG (Food Is Good) is a delightful offering spearheaded by Michael Lata, formerly of Anson. He brings an equally pleasing menu to FIG, inspired by his frequent travels in France, where fine dining is a way of life. Local farmers supply the freshest ingredients at peak flavor, and the results are reflected in every meal served. Vegetarians love the fresh plate of the day's best produce specially prepared by the chef for maximum enjoyment. The ever-changing menu frequently includes a tomato and onion tart with creamy goat cheese or steamed Capers Inlet clams as starters. Look for Keegan-Filion Farms chicken liver pâté—or if you like, have corn-flour-dusted snowy grouper with Yukon Gold puree. Seasonal desserts like Edisto Meyer lemon pudding make a rewarding finale. Wines—domestic and imported—are plentiful and served by the glass or bottle. The cocktail and beer menus offer selections for the more adventurous. **232 Meeting St., (843) 805-5900, eatatfig.com.**

Husk Restaurant. Garnering accolades right from the get go, Husk was named *Bon Appétit*'s best new restaurant in America in 2011. *Southern Living* readers felt the same way. And what makes it so good? Well, maybe it's due to the James Beard

Award-winning Chef Sean Brock and Lowcountry native Executive Chef Travis Grimes, who explore what they call "ingredient-driven cuisine" using heirloom food products from the bounty of the South. This means that the menu changes daily but might include fare such as Blue Ridge bison short rib with sweet onion relish, Ambrose spinach, and cider glacé or cornmeal-dusted North Carolina catfish with fried cabbage, green tomato chow chow, and Appalachian tomato gravy. Who could resist a Southern side dish like Carolina Gold rice and field peas Hoppin' John or a skillet of corn bread with Tennessee bacon? To satisfy that down-South sweet tooth, finish off with butterscotch trifle or warm apple cinnamon coffee cake. No wonder Husk continues to delight. **76 Queen St., (843) 577-2500, huskrestaurant.com.**

Oak Steakhouse. What locals remember as the little luncheon eatery called BJ's took on a whole new identity when the 1840s-era building (originally a bank) went through a $3 million renovation and expansion, which took seven months to complete. When done, the stage was set for high drama, and a New York-style steak house par excellence opened its doors. This is an upscale source for steaks, chops, seafood, and even vegetarian specialties—all served with flair. They use only prime Angus beef, and you may order from a number of specially prepared sauces to complement your selection. Among the favorite starters is the steak tartare with quail egg, herb aioli, cornichons, and crostini. The marinated sixteen-ounce boneless rib eye is a popular steak for the hearty appetite. For those not in a beef state of mind, there's the pan-seared crispy local chicken, and jumbo lump crab cakes. The wine selection is served up from a vault that in an earlier life held Confederate bonds. There's also a tasty bar menu to accompany one of their specialty cocktails or martinis. Valet parking is offered along busy Broad Street, which is a welcome gesture of true hospitality. Reservations are definitely called for, as space is limited. **17 Broad St., (843) 722-4220, oaksteakhousecharleston.com.**

Peninsula Grill. The restaurant in the Planters Inn is the Peninsula Grill, an elegantly simple and altogether comfortable dining experience that has "extraordinary" written all over it. For instance, half the menu is devoted to the Champagne Bar, which offers an Old World selection of champagnes by the glass and a list of mixed cocktails that reads like a page from Noel Coward's *Private Lives*. The Champagne Bar menu includes a full selection of oysters, lobster (fresh from Maine), and other seafood specialties. Try the roasted rack of lamb or the pan-seared Carolina trout. The steaks, chops, and accompanying side dishes are equally fine. A courteous and capable staff attends to diners. As for wine, there's an extensive list—mostly from France and California. Several labels are available by the glass. Their Ultimate Coconut Cake is so popular that they will ship one overnight anywhere in the United States. Reservations are suggested. **112 North Market St., (843) 723-0700, peninsulagrill.com.**

Dining Near Charleston's Historic Waterfront

Dining with a water view always kicks the ambience up a notch or two, and with all the rivers and creeks winding around Charleston several restaurants serve it up in style. Here are a few of some popular ones with a couple in downtown Charleston, and others a bit farther afield. Some even have docking if arriving by boat, and one is actually on a boat that cruises the harbor while dancing and dining. That salt air always makes for a healthy appetite!

The Boathouse at Breach Inlet. Right on the stretch of water known as Breach Inlet, is this unique restaurant with spectacular sunset views. The decor is nautical, but nice, and the menu includes pastas, broiled and fried seafood, and house specialties such as the Boathouse crab cake with green Tabasco sauce and roasted corn salsa, and the fresh catch of the day. The sides are as interesting as the entrees. Look for stone-ground grits, blue- cheese coleslaw, and collard greens. Parking is free. **101 Palm Blvd., Isle of Palms, (843) 886-8000, boathouserestaurants.com.**

California Dreaming Restaurant and Bar. You can go to California Dreaming by car or by boat (yes, you can tie up at a dock), and it's always an adventure. The kids pretend it's an old fort (although it isn't), and the views of the Ashley River are mesmerizing. The restaurant and the bar do an incredible, nonstop business year-round. The interior is colorfully decorated with flags and divided into two dining levels, with seating for 260 (and the place is often full). The little ones are welcome and can order from a special menu. Patrons really go crazy for the soft, buttery croissants and the house salad (topped with eggs, almonds, ham, and bacon—almost a meal in itself). All fish is fresh and local, and the burgers, ribs, and house special prime rib are popular. A decadent dessert list includes the fabulous apple walnut cinnamon pie. Reservations are suggested. **1 Ashley Pointe Dr., (843) 766-1644, californiadreaming.com.**

Charleston Crab House. On the Intracoastal Waterway along Wappoo Creek, is the Charleston Crab House. This restaurant specializes in "Southern seafood" and their crab pot, steamed garlic crabs (cooked until they are red, then placed before you for what locals call a "crab crack"), is a favorite. There is a raw bar, and outside tables for dining are close to the water. You can arrive by boat and moor at the restaurant dock, and they will even prepare your own catch. No reservations are necessary. There's a "fiddler crab" (kids) menu, and Mom and Dad may enjoy frozen tropical drinks. **145 Wappoo Creek Dr., (843) 795-1963, charlestoncrabhouse.com. Also, 41 South Market St., (843) 853-2900.**

Fleet Landing Restaurant. Curiously, there are not a lot of waterfront dining establishments on Peninsula Charleston. Fleet Landing addresses that problem. Their building juts out over the marsh and water on a reinforced pier offering up a wonderful view of Charleston Harbor and all its shipping and boating activities. This 6,000-square-foot concrete structure built in 1942 served as a debarkation point for U.S. Navy sailors, thus the name "Fleet Landing." Today the chic maritime decor and classic, yet contemporary, Southern seafood menu make a perfect combination for a fun dining experience. Dine inside or hit the deck. Some of the regular menu items include Carolina lump crab cakes, chargrilled rib eye, and pan-seared tilapia. Seasonal items may include tempura-fried soft-shell crab, bacon-wrapped shad roe over creamy grits, and Johns Island tomatoes. They have a nice selection of regular and specialty beers, creative cocktails, and interesting martinis. Some parking is available in their lot in front or nearby metered parking or a parking garage across the street. **186 Concord St., (843) 722-8100, fleetlanding.net.**

Marina Variety Store & Restaurant. Enjoy good food as well as a magnificent view of the Ashley River at what regulars call the Variety Store. Offering breakfast, lunch, and dinner in a very casual setting, the restaurant serves basic, good food. For instance, you can order eggs, bacon, and toast for breakfast before church and come back for a tuna salad sandwich and cup of okra soup after the noon regatta. If you want to return that night, a dinner of fresh fish with red rice and a salad is a distinct possibility. Spirits are available, and children are welcome. Take-out is a popular option for City Marina guests and locals. **17 Lockwood Dr., City Marina, (843) 723-6325, varietystorerestaurant.com.**

The Ocean Room. The signature dining venue at The Sanctuary, Kiawah's luxury hotel and spa complex, is the Ocean Room. Up a dramatic staircase from the lobby is a handsome bar that introduces the Ocean Room's dining adventure, where expansive views overlooking the Atlantic give the place its name. Elegant decor and excellent service are expected here—the cuisine is New American with an emphasis on beef entrees, and presentation is one of the points of focus. The ever-changing menu includes some favorites like the lobster bisque with Madeira sabayon, or the shrimp cocktail with spiced Palmetto Lager-poached shrimp. Favorite entrees include the seared Atlantic salmon and the Ocean Room filet with house-made béarnaise. Of course, the sommelier directs guests through an extensive wine list to recommend the perfect accompanying vintage. The pastry chef presents a tantalizing array of fantastic desserts for the Ocean Room's finale. Reservations are definitely recommended. **1 Sanctuary Beach Dr., (843) 768-6253, (800) 654-2924, thesanctuary.com.**

Red's Ice House. A casual spot where diners get a view of Shem Creek, Red's Ice House is a landmark along the popular restaurant row on both sides of the creek. You'll enjoy oysters, scallops, fish, and shrimp, as well as landlubber fare such as hamburgers and chicken. But make no mistake— right-off-the-boat shrimp and fish are the main draw here. Red's is right on the water, where shrimp boats dock and boaters cruise, to see and be seen. Red's colorful atmosphere makes this a happenin' place for young singles, especially on weekend nights. **98 Church St., (843) 388-0003, redsicehouse.com. The Bohicket Marina location (1882 Andell Bluff Rd., 843-518-5515) has a spectacular dockside setting, too.**

SpiritLine Dinner Cruise. Dining and dancing aboard this ninety-six-foot luxury tour boat while cruising historic Charleston Harbor make for one of those quintessential Charleston experiences. The *Spirit of Carolina* serves a three-course meal of she-crab soup, house salad, and a choice of five entrees such as grilled rib-eye steak, porterhouse-cut pork, chicken, or seafood (also vegetarian and vegan) per prior request. All menu items are served with a nod toward the Lowcountry tradition of cooking. The boat makes its rounds up and down the waterways at sundown and is always a lot of fun. Live music and dancing are part of the nightly bill of fare. Entertainment is provided by a live band, which can perform jazz, blues, shag, and country music as per your request. *Spirit of Carolina* is part of the Fort Sumter Tours group and conveniently departs from the docks at Patriots Point Naval and Maritime Museum, where there's parking at the clearly marked boarding dock for a cash fee. **40 Patriots Point Rd., Mount Pleasant, (843) 722-2628, (800) 789-3678, spiritlinecruises. com. Rates and schedules change seasonally and tickets must be purchased in advance. A cash bar is available onboard.**

More Places to See

Charleston Tea Plantation. There's more to your breakfast cup of tea than meets the eye (or the tongue as the case may be). Just how much goes into the making of tea is demonstrated at the Charleston Tea Plantation on Wadmalaw Island. A bit off the beaten track, but well worth seeing, is this fascinating, unexpected attraction featuring a processing plant, retail shop, and vast fields containing hundreds of thousands of tea plants (*Camellia sinensis*). Visitors follow the tender tea leaves being processed from harvest through packaging in a carefully controlled environment. This is an unusual tourist experience, but a unique one as this is America's only tea plantation. Even though nature doesn't allow harvesting every day, the entire black-tea-manufacturing process is shown on three large screens displayed along the viewing gallery. Guests can sample tea and shop for distinctive teapots and other fine items in the pleasant Tea Shoppe. If you like you can take a forty-minute relaxing ride through majestic live oaks to the fields on the Charleston Tea Plantation Trolley. **6617 Maybank Hwy. (SC 700, across the Ashley River) (843) 559-0383, charlestonteaplantation.com.**

Drayton Hall. Not a tour of a reconstructed working plantation or the collected decorative arts from a bygone era, Drayton Hall offers an adventure in architecture. Yes, architecture and a great deal more. If for no other reason, Drayton Hall should be seen and experienced as the sole survivor of the 1865 rampage by Union troops, who looted and burned nearly every other plantation house along the Ashley River. But, there is more to Drayton Hall, as it also stands as a survivor of many other changes, influences, forces, and times. It was built between 1738 and 1742 as the country seat (primary home) of John Drayton (1716–1779). The house is considered one of the oldest and finest examples of Georgian-Palladian architecture in America. The structure remains almost untouched as an eloquent statement about eighteenth-century thinking, craftsmanship, technology, and design. It's one of the few sites left in colonial America so pure, unaltered, and uncompromising. Visitors will find the Drayton Hall story—how it all came to pass—interpreted by a small group of professional guides who lead you through 250 years of time, family genealogy, architectural history, and a smattering of the economic and social realities of the plantation system. The staff has

The old plantation house at Drayton Hall.
© ISTOCK.COM/CODE6D

recorded oral histories of the Drayton family as well as the African Americans so closely associated with the house and its survival. A map is provided to visitors for a self-guided nature walk through the Drayton property including marsh, riverfront, and forest areas. Major portions of the nature trails are wheelchair accessible. The National Trust for Historic Preservation now owns the site. Admission prices include a professionally guided tour of the historic house and a self-guided tour of the grounds, including the African-American cemetery and their interactive Connections program. **3380 Ashley River Rd., (843) 769-2600, draytonhall. org. A written tour in English, French, or German can be purchased.**

Magnolia Plantation and Gardens. This is where Thomas Drayton Jr., father of Drayton Hall's John Drayton, settled when he came to Charles Towne in 1679. Early on, the home that Drayton, a successful English planter from the island of Barbados, built for himself and his family was destroyed by fire. The house built to replace it was subsequently burned by Union troops in 1865. The present structure is said to have been a Drayton family hunting lodge that was moved down the Ashley River in 1873 and placed atop the foundations of the old plantation house. Magnolia Plantation is the original (and continuing) home of the Drayton family, now owned and managed by a twelfth-generation descendant. It is famous for its expansive, informal, English-style gardens, which are the legacy of the Reverend John Grimke-Drayton, the plantation's owner during the American Civil War. Look for the garden called Flowerdale. Here is Magnolia's earliest garden area (planted in the late 1680s), and it was possibly the inspiration for Grimke-Drayton's larger, more ambitious plan a century-and-a-half later. Today, the gardens boast 250 varieties of azaleas and 900 varieties of camellias. These, plus many other flowers added through the years, keep Magnolia Gardens in colorful bloom all year long. Its most spectacular season, however, is spring, when the dazzling, vibrant azalea colors seem to vibrate on the landscape as far as the eye can see. Visitors can get an overview of the property in a twelve-minute video on the plantation's history shown at regular intervals in the orientation theater.

Magnolia Plantation offers additional activities for nature lovers. Canoes can be rented to glide through the eerie beauty of its 125-acre waterfowl refuge. There are walking and bicycle trails, plus a wildlife observation tower that's very popular with bird-watchers. There's an herb garden, a

The gardens at Magnolia Plantation were first opened to the public in the early 1870s and are the oldest unrestored gardens in America.
© LYNN WHITT/ SHUTTERSTOCK.COM

horticultural maze, newly opened antebellum slave cabins, a typical Ashley River rice barge, and even a petting zoo for children (as well as adults). You'll find picnic areas, a snack shop, and a gift shop there, too. The Audubon Swamp Garden encompasses a sixty-acre, black-water cypress and tupelo swamp. The visitor has the opportunity to see an otherwise inaccessible natural area via boardwalks, dikes, and bridges that provide an intimate view of the horticultural beauty and wildlife, including a few alligators. The swamp garden gets its name from the great nineteenth-century American naturalist and wildlife artist John James Audubon, who visited Magnolia in search of water bird specimens during his many lengthy stays in Charleston. This attraction is a one-hour self-guided walking tour. **3550 Ashley River Rd., (843) 571-1266, (800) 367-3517, magnoliaplantation. com. Additional fees added for the Plantation House, Nature Train/Boat, Slavery to Freedom tour, and Audubon Swamp.**

Middleton Place. Middleton is one of the Lowcountry's most famous plantations and another National Historic Landmark along the rich and fascinating Ashley River. This was the home of Henry Middleton, president of the First Continental Congress, and his son Arthur, a signer of the Declaration of Independence. The sheer size and scope of Middleton's gardens tell a great deal about the man and his grand vision. The twelve-acre greensward, with its grazing sheep and strutting peacocks, creates an unforgettable image for the first-time visitor. Not to be missed is the view of the Ashley River from the high terraces of the gardens. The

green grass ripples down the hillside to the graceful butterfly lakes below. This bucolic, pastoral scene belies the frenzy of activity and the vast labor force needed to maintain this busy world. On the Middleton Place grounds is Eliza's House, an actual freedman's dwelling. At the lively plantation stable-yards, with active displays of day-to-day life, you'll find a blacksmith, a potter, weavers, and carpenters all busy at work and eager to explain and demonstrate their skills. The main house, built sometime before 1741, was—like Magnolia's—burned in 1865 by Union troops. The south flanker building (added about 1755) was least damaged by the fire, and it was essentially rebuilt in the early years of the twentieth century in its present form. Just past the rice mill, a path leads into the forest and up a hill to the Inn at Middleton Place, a fifty-five-room riverside oasis for discerning overnight travelers. With vine-covered stucco and unblinking modern glass

Middleton Place boasts some of the most beautiful and intricate gardens in the Lowcountry.
© VISIONSOFMAINE/ SHUTTERSTOCK.COM

walls, each suite looks out over a green, woodland setting or the quiet waters of the Ashley River. **4300 Ashley River Rd., (843) 556-6020, (800) 782-3608, middletonplace.org. House tour admission adds a fee per person to Middleton Place rates. An optional carriage ride through the property is additional. A Spend-The-Day discounted admission combines all three activities. A combination ticket to the Edmonston-Alston House located downtown is available. The Restaurant at Middleton Place serves authentic Lowcountry cuisine. There's no admission charge for entry to the property after 5:30 PM with dinner reservations. (843) 266-7477.**

Mepkin Abbey. On an historic rice plantation, once the home of American Revolutionary War patriot Henry Laurens, there is now a beautiful oasis called Mepkin Abbey. There, a stalwart band of monks live, work, and pray in a religious compound they've occupied since 1949. Its setting on the quiet banks of the Cooper River first attracted publishing giant Henry Luce (*Time* and *Life* magazines), along with his diplomat wife, Claire Booth Luce, in the 1930s. Their winter retreat was designed by Edward Durell Stone and was a popular stop for many famous intelligentsia of that era.

In 1949 after the unexpected death of the Luces' daughter, the estate was transferred to the Roman Catholic Church and in turn, the monks of Gethsemani from Kentucky. This highly disciplined sect belongs to the Cistercian Order popularly known as Trappist. The monks dedicate their lives to study and prayer in the belief that entreating God for mercy benefits the whole world. To sustain themselves the monks cultivate and sell organic mushrooms and garden compost as a business enterprise. The atmosphere of Mepkin Abbey is contemplative and refreshing. Individuals with something to resolve internally may go to the abbey for a time of retreat and meditation by special arrangement in advance. Guests are expected to fit in with the rhythmic schedule of monastic life while there. Casual day visitors may check in with the guest master at the abbey's reception center and gift shop for tours of the chapel, library, and gardens. At Christmastime the display of crèches from all over the world attracts appreciative crowds and has become an annual pilgrimage for many families. **1098 Mepkin Abbey Rd., (843) 761-8509, mepkinabbey.org.**

The gardens at Mepkin Abbey

Glossary

As a quick reference for those who don't happen to keep the eight basic architectural styles of historic Charleston constantly top-of-mind, the following definitions (courtesy of the Historic Charleston Foundation and the National Trust for Historic Preservation) are offered:

Art Deco is exemplified in the highly stylized look that many American buildings took during the years between the world wars, roughly 1920 to 1940. Look for decorative panels, narrow windows, flat roofs, and multicolored bands. Charleston's most outstanding example is the beautifully restored Riviera Theater, 225–227 King St.

Classical Revival is the architectural return to the lines and look of ancient Greece (and later, Rome). It was popular in America from about 1820 to 1875. Look for large, heavy columns and capitals, temple pediments, triglyphs and guttae, and all the other details in classic Greek architectural order. In Charleston, a great example is Beth Elohim Synagogue, 90 Hasell St.

Colonial refers to the period from 1690 to 1740. Look for a very low foundation, beaded clapboard siding, a high-pitched gable roof (sometimes with flared eaves), hipped dormers, and raised panel shutters. A good Charlestonian example is the John Lining House, 106 Broad St. at King St.

Federal is the American architectural style seen chiefly between the years 1790 and 1820. In England, the style is called Adam, in reference to the English-Irish architect Robert Adam. Look for geometric rooms, ironwork balconies, a low-pitched roof, decorative bands around interior rooms, exterior trim, spiral stairs, and elliptical fanlights. The Nathaniel Russell House, 51 Meeting St., is a fine Charleston example.

Georgian refers to the architectural style popular in England during the reign of Anne and the four Georges. Here in America, the style is generally assigned to the years 1700 to 1790. Look for a hipped roof, box chimneys, triangular pediments (often with oval lights), columns, a raised basement, and a belt course between floors. An excellent Charleston example is the Miles Brewton House, 27 King St.

Gothic Revival refers to the period between 1850 and 1885, when many American building designs borrowed from the up-reaching lines of western European architecture between the twelfth and sixteenth centuries. Look for pointed arches, buttresses, stone tracery, and finials. At 136 Church St., the French Huguenot Church exemplifies this style.

Italianate is shown in the popular building style seen here between 1830 and 1900. Look for paired brackets and round head arches, balustrades, a low-pitched roof, and the loggia (or veranda). A classic Charleston example is the Colonel John Algernon Sydney Ashe House, 26 South Battery.

Victorian refers, of course, to England's Queen Victoria, who reigned from 1836 to 1901. In American architecture, however, it was a popular style between the years 1860 and 1915. Look for a multi-gabled roof, elaborate wood bracket work (sometimes called gingerbread), turrets, and roof decorations. A rare Charleston example is the Sottile House, on the College of Charleston campus at Green St.

Bibliography and Suggested Reading

Chesnut, Mary Boykin. *A Diary from Dixie*. Edited by Ben Ames Williams. Cambridge, Mass.: Harvard University Press, 1980.

Edgar, Walter, ed. *South Carolina: A History*. Columbia, S.C.: University of South Carolina Press, 1998.

Edgar, Walter, ed. *The South Carolina Encyclopedia*. Columbia, S.C.: University of South Carolina Press, 2006.

Fraser, Walter J. Jr. *Charleston! Charleston! The History of a Southern City*. Columbia, S.C.: University of South Carolina Press, 1989.

Moore, Margaret H. *Complete Charleston: A Guide to the Architecture, History & Gardens of Charleston and the Low Country*. Charleston, S.C.: TM Photography, Inc., 2000.

Perry, Lee Davis and McLaughlin, J. Michael. *It Happened in South Carolina*. Guilford, Conn.: The Globe Pequot Press, 2011.

Perry, Lee Davis. *More Than Petticoats: Remarkable South Carolina Women*. Guilford, Conn.: The Globe Pequot Press, 2009.

Perry, Lee Davis. *Insiders' Guide to Charleston*. Guilford, Conn.: The Globe Pequot Press, 2015.

Perry, Lee Davis and McLaughlin, J. Michael. *South Carolina Curiosities*. Guilford, Conn.: The Globe Pequot Press, 2011.

Rogers, George C. Jr. *Charleston in the Age of the Pinckneys*. Columbia, SC: University of South Carolina Press, 1980.

South Carolina Information Highway Website, sciway.net.

Index

121

124

Index

About the Author

Lee Davis Perry was raised in Charleston and returned there in 1987 to focus on a freelance marketing and advertising career. She is the author of *Insiders' Guide to Charleston* and *More Than Petticoats: Remarkable South Carolina Women* (Globe Pequot).